The Barefoot Gypsy

The Barefoot Gypsy

A Gluten and Dairy-Free Cookbook

Easy to follow, healthy, and nutritious recipes that you and your family with love. I hope this book inspires you to live a life that honors both the earth and your body.

By Whitney Robinson

Foreword

Let me start off by saying that my human is an amazing cook. I am there watching her make every meal, just praying for a dropped scrap. She hasn't been cooking for many years like most humans who are writing cookbooks, but I can promise you this book is filled with simple, delicious, gluten and dairy-free recipes.

She got into cooking when she moved out to California. She went from being single and living alone to being a stepmom of three and an animal mom to over fifteen. With that many mouths to feed, she had to learn quickly. With her new found gluten and dairy intolerance she had to become creative when cooking. She threw out all of the gluten and dairy in the house and began to experiment. She came up with some really rad stuff, but she would always get frustrated because she would forget to write down and save the recipe. So that is when she got the brilliant idea to put this book together.

My mom's number one priority is to feed our whole family healthy and delicious food, but she doesn't want it taking up all of her time. She tries to use the fewest dishes possible, and most meals can be made in thirty minutes or under. A lot of things she makes can be prepped on Sunday and used throughout the week, like my food and treats, as well as human food like nut milk, desserts, and snacks.

I can't wait for y'all to try these recipes, and I hope you love them as much as I do. I've tried just about everything, you know. I have my own seat at the table.

Ruff Ruff,

Berry

Table of Contents

About the Author

Hi, I'm Whitney Robinson. I live in Encinitas, CA, a beachside town in sunny San Diego County, with my husband, Adam, and three stepkids, Asher, Kellan, and Reed. We live on a little ranch with six dogs: Ruqa, Berry, Tazzy, Pickle, Oreo and BJ. We also have nine chickens, a pig, a sulcata tortoise, and a lively hive of honeybees. A portion of our backyard is covered by an edible garden, where I spend a lot of time working and harvesting the food we eat.

In addition to nurturing our garden, I also handle the leasing for our commercial real estate company, RPG, and design beautiful, handmade crystal jewelry. At the end of 2019, I opened Gypsy Feather, a boutique in Encinitas, to sell my jewelry and other finds from around the world. During covid I added a fun Gypsy Feather athletic and athleisure line which has been a huge success. You can check it all out at Gypsy-Feather.com.

When I am not working, designing, or taking care of the kids and animals, you can usually find me in the kitchen or working out. With five human mouths to feed, I do a lot of cooking and experimenting. Each week I prepare our nut milk, dog food, dog treats, nut butter, desserts, and even lotion for the family. We are all happily gluten and dairy-free, so I prioritize having some convenient and healthy things in the fridge.

As you have probably gathered, I am a very busy person. I've built my life around a healthy and productive routine that serves both me and my family. Flip through the pages here for a plethora of tips and tricks to start building your own wellness routines, getting closer to nature, and living a life that honors both the earth and your body.

- Whitney

Introduction

Do you ever get stomach pains, feel congested, or just feel sluggish after you eat? If so, the problem might be food related. Food is supposed to be a fun and enjoyable experience, but that isn't always the case. I've had lots of ups and downs with food throughout my life, as I am sure everyone has. I cut out dairy, gluten, and alcohol about two years ago, and I feel amazing. I know this sounds extreme, and if you would have told me a few years ago that I'd be doing this, I would have laughed at you and called you crazy. I did it in phases and have made lots of adjustments in my cooking to help fill any cravings I had. You will still be able to eat fried chicken, ranch dressing, cheesecake, and many other things that seem off-limits when eliminating gluten and dairy. There are times when I break the rules—if I'm on vacation or out for a special night—and that's ok. This is not a crash diet; it's a lifestyle, and it is made to be enjoyed, not to feel like a hold-back.

I know there are lots of people out there who are having issues with their bodies and are searching for answers. I'm not a doctor, just a regular, everyday human, trying to shine some light on the issues I had and cured by cutting out certain foods, hoping that it might help a few people out along the way. And if you're feeling good and just wanting to find some new healthy recipes, that's okay too.

This book will take you through my journey with food, give you over 130 delicious gluten and dairy-free recipes, teach you some tips & tricks on how to prep things and make cooking at home fun and easy, and even show you how to cut down on waste by creating a compost pile.

I am very efficient with everything I do in life, cooking included. I make meals that are quick and easy with the fewest dishes possible. It doesn't matter if they look perfect; they still taste amazing. I want you to be able to feed your family healthy, home-cooked meals that don't take up all your free time.

Throughout this book, I use Kerrygold grass-fed butter and ghee in a some of my recipes, but if you can't tolerate these you can always sub dairy-free butter or coconut oil. Typically, if someone has a dairy intolerance, it's an allergy to casein (a protein in milk) or lactose. Ghee contains neither, and grass-fed butter is very low in lactose, so they're tolerated in a lot of dairy-free diets. If you're super sensitive, please sub out for the dairy-free options.

My Journey

I have been unknowingly battling food for all of my life. This may sound crazy, but it took me until my thirties to figure out what was going on with my body and to be able to fix it. Now that I look back on it, there were so many signs that pointed to a dairy intolerance, but at the time we had no idea.

From the time I was born, I had what the doctors told us were digestive issues. Breast milk would make me projectile vomit. My parents took me to countless doctors to find answers, but no one could give us any. They told my mom to stop breastfeeding and to switch to formula. She did, and she tried many, but the symptoms continued. Many tests were done, but they always came back free and clear. The doctor finally told us that as long as I was gaining weight, not to worry, that I would eventually grow out of it, so that's what we did.

Throughout my first year, I threw up almost every day. When I switched off of formula to baby food and milk, things got a little bit better. Instead of throwing up every day, it was a few times a week. But hey, this was progress, right?

I grew up in the '80s when food allergies were unheard of, and eating canned, boxed, and processed foods was very popular. Every morning, I would go to school on an empty stomach because eating breakfast then riding in the car made me sick. I would bring a small snack from home to eat in the nurse's office to hold me over until lunch. I would often buy lunch at school, which was full of gluten and dairy and was always served with a carton of milk. For dinner we had chicken or beef with canned veggies and boxed Rice A Roni. I drank 2% milk with every meal and had lots of fruits, cheeses, and sugary snacks. I remember eating spaghetti noodles or white rice with sugar on top for a dessert many nights. My friends always loved to come over because there was a candy jar in every room, and my mom was always making cakes and cookies. Little did I or my family know, the things I was eating were killing me inside.

When I was in elementary school, there were lots of random things that would make me sick: I couldn't eat and ride in the car; my mom couldn't wear perfume; I would get nauseous when I got really hot; or sometimes it would just come out of nowhere for no apparent reason. There were many times when I was walking down the hall in elementary school and my stomach pain would be so bad it would stop me in my tracks. I would have to hunch over until the pain passed, then I would continue on with what I was doing.

Being nauseated was part of my life; it would pop up here and there, and by "here and there" I mean several times a week, usually at the worst times, like right before a talent show or in the middle of class. I got really good at managing it. I would know when it was coming and have enough time to run to the bathroom so that I wasn't causing a scene.

On top of all that, I would get strep throat every year, probably because I was malnourished and thus had a weak immune system. It would last on and off for about five months. I would power through, but a lot of the time, that would make me not hungry, causing me to be skin and bones. My knees were the biggest part of my legs and often people asked my mom if I was sick.

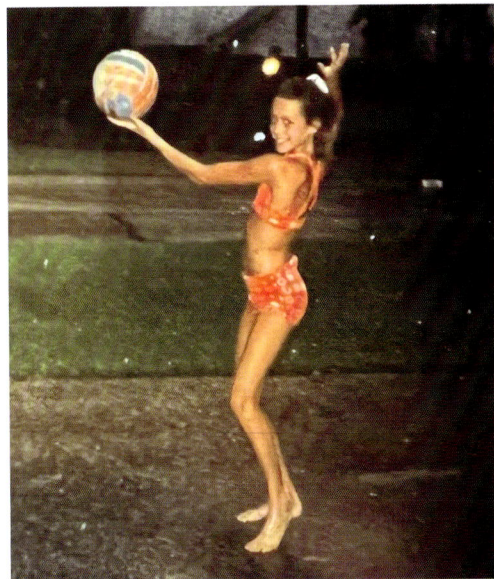

When I was about twelve years old, I got my tonsils and adenoids taken out. Once those were gone, I started to feel better. In an attempt to help me gain weight, my mom would make me a chocolate milkshake every night before bed. Little did she know that the milkshakes were feeding my problem. Even though at this point I had outgrown the frequent vomiting, all of the dairy was causing me to have congestion and stomach pain. My congestion got so bad that I started carrying a bottle of Afrin with me everywhere I went to help relieve my stuffy nose.

High school was much better, I was starting to gain weight and look healthy. I could eat just about anything without throwing up, and my stomach pains were not as bad—or maybe I was just used to them. I had quit drinking nightly milkshakes, and they didn't serve milk with lunch in high school. I was craving more healthy, fresh foods, like sandwiches with tons of veggies on them and salads. I played sports year-round and was very active and energetic. My congestion was the only thing that was bothering me, but I had Afrin in my back pocket, which cleared it up in seconds, so I was golden. I was happy to be able to live more freely and be feeling much better.

I went off to college where I ate like crap and drank like a fish. I worked out and stayed in shape, but when I look back at photos, my face and body were puffy, and I always had a stuffy nose. My favorite drink was Leinenkugel's Sunset Wheat, a heavy wheat beer—go figure. Like a typical college kid, I would eat Jack in the Box tacos with buttermilk ranch at 2 a.m. and sleep until I needed to wake up and make it to class. College was a ton of fun, but I am glad those unhealthy days are behind me.

When I left college and moved to Austin. I became more cautious about what I was eating. I thought that a low-fat, low-calorie diet was good for you. I was living on my own and traveling for work. I was opening up new locations for a sports bar all over Texas, Oklahoma, and North Carolina. This meant traveling to the new locations while living in a motel for five to six weeks and eating out for every meal. I worked out when I could, but I worked long days, so it didn't happen often. When the location was up and running, I would head back home and bartend in Austin until it was time to hit the road again.

One night when I was working, a guy made a comment to me about my weight. I had gained about fifteen pounds, and obviously he noticed. He asked me when my baby was due. It sent me into a whirl of emotions. This was a turning point for me in my diet. From that night on, I tracked everything I ate, down to the ounce of mustard. I was obsessed with it and it caused me to have a bad relationship with food. If I was close to the calorie limit for the day, I would stop eating, even if I was still hungry. The foods I was filling my body with were not nutritious, filling foods. Since I didn't cook, I was grabbing quick things, heating up premade meals, and grabbing food to go. In about a month or two, I got down to my lowest weight. I didn't feel good, I wasn't eating enough, my energy was low, and it was something that I could not maintain. For the next couple of years, I went through fad diets that never really worked. I would still get stomach pains, I developed really bad heartburn, and my nose was always stuffy. Yep, that Afrin was still on me at all times.

In 2013, I moved to Southeast Asia. I bought a one-way ticket and packed a three month supply of Nexium and a few bottles of Afrin; those were the essentials. What would I do without them? About a month into the trip, I was able to throw out all of my Nexium. I was no longer getting heartburn, and my sinuses were starting to clear up. I thought this was due to being halfway across the world with a change in scenery (no more allergies), but now that I look back on it, Vietnam, Cambodia, Indonesia, Thailand—none of those countries eat dairy and all of their food is extremely fresh. When I took away the dairy, I instantly felt better. Dairy has been the root cause of most my problems since the day I was born.

In 2014, when I returned from Asia, I was still blind to the fact that I had a dairy intolerance. I ate what seemed to be healthy, but everything was packed with gluten and dairy, and I wasn't getting enough protein. Most of the time I ate for fuel; I didn't cook much. I would stop and get a meal at Whole Foods or Chipotle, or a turkey burgers from P. Terry's. I would snack all day long, because at the time, I was working from home and my fridge and pantry were just steps away from my couch office. My roommate was a vegetarian and loved cheese, so we would both eat cheese all the time. We would go out a few times a week, and of course I was drinking Blue Moon or some other kind of wheat beer. I was eating things that seemed decently healthy, but I didn't realize they were causing so much inflammation and pain.

In 2018, I moved to California, got married, and hoped that the change of residence would make what I still thought were allergies go away like it did when I was living in Asia. But guess what? It didn't. About a year in, I went to an allergy doctor and learned that I had a wheat intolerance. I cut out gluten, hoping that would be the answer to all of my issues. After a about a month, my stomach pains started to decrease, but I was still congested.

It wasn't until March 2019, when my acupuncturist recommended I go to a holistic chiropractor, that the rest fell into place. I made an appointment and told him about my ongoing sinus and stomachache problems. He did a muscle test, where he held up colors for me to look at while he pressed on my arm (sounds crazy, I know). After the test, he told me that I was dairy-intolerant. He said to quit eating dairy and your sinus and stomach problems would all go away. Leaving there, laughing, and thinking he was full of it, I promised myself I would do it for at least three days. Except for the time I was in Asia, I don't think I had ever gone three days without eating dairy in my entire lifetime.

At that point in my life, I was cooking healthy meals from our garden and eating at least a block of cheese a day. I loved cheese boards. When we had guests, I would always create a giant cheese board and would be snacking on it all throughout the day. I would sometimes even make one for dinner because I loved them so much. I knew it would be hard to go three days, but there is no way I would be able to cut out dairy for good—no way! I sucked it up and did it for those three long days. By day four, it was like magic: My stomach was free of pain, my nose was clear, and I couldn't believe it.

I've been on the dairy and gluten-free journey for about two years now, and I've never felt better. Honestly, I don't miss cheese nearly as much as I thought I would. I try to stay away from processed sugars and alcohol, but sometimes I do eat them or have a drink. This lifestyle change has me feeling great, and I am in the best shape of my life. I feel and look younger than I did ten years ago.

Over the past two years, I've learned a lot. I've made lots of really good meals and some that have ended up in the trash. I've come up with several tricks to make things more efficient and recipes that help cut the cravings for dairy and gluten.

I've tried to add in sheep or goat cheese to the mix, but every time I do, the next day I have mucus in my throat, and I feel sluggish. My body does not do well with any kind of cheese, but if you're someone who is able to add these in, more power to you. I've added goat cheese into some of these recipes as an option, so if you're able to have it, go for it.

Because I was curious, I recently did a food sensitivity test with a naturopathic doctor. They take a blood sample, and it comes back with a whole list of things that you shouldn't be eating. The results came in, and sure enough, I shouldn't be eating cow's milk, goat's milk, sheep's milk, spelt, wheat, or rye. So I am sensitive to any and all milk products and all gluten products. Thirty-three years later, a test finally came back with the answers.

I love feeling full of energy and ready to go in the mornings, a feeling that takes me easily through my very full day. We also love to travel, and when we do, this routine is not always possible. I believe that breaking away and having fun does no harm. When vacation time comes around, and you want to have that delicious cheese platter, cold beer, or yummy ice cream, go for it! When I am on vacation, I sleep in and break the rules. I want to be able to enjoy meals and drinks with friends without having to modify every little thing. Treat yourself! Then, get back to your gluten and dairy-free lifestyle when you get home. It should never feel like you're missing out on life. You'll be adding more to your life, and, in reality, gaining time because you're sleeping efficiently and being as productive as possible.

My Routine

Every morning I wake up at around 6:30 a.m. It doesn't matter what time I went to bed, my mental clock—or maybe it's the dogs licking my face wanting to go potty—wakes me up. I have not always been a morning person. In fact, when I was younger, my mom could never get me out of bed. I would sleep all day if she would let me. More than likely, this was due to my body feeling bogged down from food that was causing so many internal issues, and I was never getting quality rest.

The first thing I do when I jump out of bed is brush my teeth and floss (so important), wash my face, use toner and moisturizer. I need to start the day off feeling fresh. Then I jump into my gym clothes, make my bed, and let the dogs out. Making your bed before leaving the room is a great habit; a clean and organized home makes things so much less stressful. I grab all of our food scraps that I've saved for the animals and take them out to feed them to the tortoise. I let the chickens out of their area to free-range, give them some treats, and I feed the pig. I take the dogs back inside and feed them my delicious homemade dog food (pg. 268).

Now it's time to take care of myself: I make thirty-two ounces of fresh celery juice each morning. My husband and I chug down sixteen ounces each. Celery juice has so many benefits: It helps with digestion and can help clear up skin problems, just to name a few. I fill a container with ice, water, and oranges, lemons, limes, or whatever I have on hand (pg. 216). The infused water sits on the counter, so I remember to drink it.

I go immediately to work out. I fill up my water bottle and add a scoop of BCAA (branched-chain amino acids) to help me work out smarter, not harder. I either go to F45 (a HIIT style group workout), for a run to the beach (about four or five miles), or do the Peloton. Once I get a good forty-five minute sweat on, I like to take a cold shower. This doesn't always happen, but I feel so refreshed after I get out of a cold shower. Then I moisturize my body with my homemade body lotion (pg. 276). If you have dry skin and have not been able to find a lotion that works or you're sick of rubbing ingredients that you can't pronounce on your body, this is your answer! It's made with only six all-natural ingredients and is also sold at Gypsy-Feather.com.

I get dressed and head to the kitchen to make a morning shake and heat up a bowl of Brodino chicken bone broth. It's seriously the best in the world, and they will ship it to you. Bone broth has tons of benefits, it helps with your joints, is a good source of vitamins A and K as well as iron, and also helps with inflammation and healing the gut. There is not a day that goes by when I am at home that this doesn't happen. I believe that my morning routine kick-starts my day so that I am full of energy for whatever curveballs life throws me.

Keeping my to-do list close by helps me make the most of my day. Midday, I take a break to make lunch. If I am needing a little pick-me-up, I'll have a matcha latte (pg. 226) for a little extra energy boost. I like to have dinner started by 6:30 p.m. because I don't like eating late, but sometimes the day gets the best of me, and I find myself cooking closer to 8 p.m.

I wind down at night by reading or watching TV for at least an hour before going to bed. My ideal bedtime would be 10:15 p.m. But there are times, especially while I'm writing this book, that I am not in bed until after midnight. I strive to get eight hours of sleep a night, but most of the time I get closer to seven hours. I'm a light sleeper, so I use a box fan and a white noise machine to drown out any external noise.

Getting good, solid sleep is so important. I use two sleep trackers to keep up with my sleep records. The first one is the Oura ring, a sensor ring you wear on your finger. It tracks exactly when you lie down, how long it takes you to fall asleep, how many times you wake up, your REM sleep, deep sleep, light sleep, and much more. All of that info goes right to an app on your phone. It gives you a sleep score every night and a readiness score every day. You are able to add in different tags and exercises to help you know what might be causing sleep disturbances. It's a great tool to help you track your sleep and see what works best for your body. Since it's on your finger, it tracks all of its data based on movement and pulse, which is great information but isn't 100% accurate. The second device I use is the Dreem.

The Dreem is a headband with sensors that you wear at night. It tracks your brain waves to tell when you're in light, deep, and REM sleep and how many times you wake up. It has a lot of the same info as the Oura ring, but it's more detailed and accurate when it comes to your sleep stages. By tracking this along with your daily activities, you're able to start seeing which habits are causing you to sleep well or which are causing sleep disturbances. It's very interesting to look at the results, see how well you slept, and use that information to help you feel your absolute best throughout the day.

There you have it—my daily routine and healthy habits. As you can see my day fluctuates based on what I have going on. Not every day is the same and you have to be able to adapt. I hope this, along with the following recipes, inspires you to find what works for you to live your healthiest life.

Suggested Appliances and Tools for the Kitchen

- Cuisinart food processor with attachments
- NutriBullet
- Cuisinart Egg Central
- Rice cooker
- Crockpot
- Vitamix
- Assorted sharp knifes
- Food processor
- Silicone spatula
- Stand or hand mixer
- Cold press or regular juicer
- Mandoline slicer
- Microplane grater
- Nut milk bag
- Garlic press
- Lime juicer
- Silicone mini muffin pan
- Silicone ice pop mold

My Fridge, Freezer and Pantry Must-Haves

FRIDGE

- **Almond/cashew milk**
- **Chicken bone broth**
- **Tamari**
- **Sriracha**
- **Fish sauce**
- **Tahini**
- **Capers**
- **Worcestershire sauce**
- **Sweet cherry peppers**
- **Mustard**: Dijon, stone-ground, yellow
- **Gluten-free noodles** (Taste Republic)

- **Mayonnaise**
- **Tofutti milk-free sour cream**
- **Pickles:** Claussen whole, sandwich slices
- **Fresh produce:** jalapeños, habaneros, serranos, peeled garlic (such a time-saver), sun-dried tomatoes, fresh ginger, fresh turmeric, mint, basil, lettuce, zucchini, carrots, napa cabbage, microgreens, alfalfa sprouts, tomatillos, kale, cucumber, dill, cilantro, celery

PROTEINS

- **Eggs:** We have our own chickens, so we are lucky enough to not have to buy store-bought eggs. It's crazy to see the difference in color when you crack a store-bought egg next to our fresh eggs. Our yolks are bright orange, and the store-bought ones are dull yellow. If you can go to the farmers market to buy eggs, do it. If you're not able to do that, buy organic, free-range eggs.

- **Air-chilled organic chicken:** I always have this in the fridge. The air-chilling process has standout benefits: It produces tastier, more tender chicken, and the breasts aren't bulked up with excess water (which would cause them to become dry when cooked). You can use it in so many recipes. I grind my own chicken from chicken breasts so I know that it's high-quality.

PROTEINS, *Cont.*

- **Wild-caught fish**: I always try to buy wild-caught fish when available. Wild-caught fish are not prone to disease or illness, because they're living in their natural habitat. The fish is usually leaner and higher in fatty acids.
- **Salami/pepperoni:** The kids love salami and pepperoni, so I always have it in the fridge for them to snack on.

FREEZER

- **Frozen fruit:** blueberries, bananas, strawberries
- **Spinach or greens of choice**
- **Chicken bone broth**

IN THE PANTRY

- **Arrowroot powder:** This was something that I bought one day for a recipe and then it sat in my pantry forever before I used it again. It acts as a thickener and is free of GMOs, so it's healthier than cornstarch. Now I use it all the time in desserts and sauces.
- **Baking soda**
- **Baking powder**
- **Health food:** collagen protein powder (Bulletproof), maca powder, matcha powder, BCAA, MCT oil
- **Flours:** almond, coconut, cassava

- **Sugars/sweets:** turbinado sugar, brown sugar, coconut sugar, vegan dark chocolate chips, raw honey, dates, maple syrup, shredded coconut, cacao
- **Butters:** coconut butter, almond butter (pg. 197), cashew butter (pg. 196), ghee, Kerrygold grass-fed butter, non-dairy butter, organic peanut butter, powdered peanut butter (Naked PB)
- **Vinegars:** apple cider, champagne, white wine, balsamic, rice, white, balsamic reduction
- **Oils:** avocado oil, extra-virgin olive oil, coconut oil, sesame oil, grapeseed oil, truffle oil, avocado oil cooking spray

IN THE PANTRY, *Cont.*

- **Spices:** ground cumin, garlic salt, garlic powder, cinnamon, Italian seasoning, dried oregano, vanilla bean powder, sesame seeds, Tajín (Mexican chili-lime mix), onion powder, chili powder, celery salt, paprika (regular and smoked), crushed red pepper, cayenne pepper, ranch seasoning, green curry powder, bay leaves, freshly ground black pepper, piperine, ground turmeric, Himalayan salt, Trader Joe's 21 Seasoning Salute, flaky sea salt

- **Nuts/Seeds:** walnuts, almonds, cashews, pistachios, pine nuts, pecans, pumpkin seeds, flaxseed, chia seeds, hemp seeds

- **Canned/Jarred foods:** crushed tomatoes, tomato paste, green curry paste, baby corn, water chestnuts, coconut milk, coconut cream, bamboo shoots, garbanzo beans, black beans, chicken stock, artichoke hearts, pumpkin, hearts of palm

- **Additional items:** vanilla extract, panko bread crumbs, gluten-free rolled oats, rice vermicelli noodles, gluten-free pretzels, white or brown rice

- **Non-food products:** reusable parchment paper, reusable beeswax food wraps, aluminum foil, lots of glass containers with lids, Mason jars, tortilla press, glass containers for nut milk, wide smoothie straws

ON THE COUNTER

- **Fresh produce:** cherry tomatoes, sweet potatoes, potatoes, lemons, limes, oranges, acorn squash, butternut squash, onions, avocados, plantains, watermelon

Health Food
Wondering what all this health food does?

BCAA

What is it? Branch chain amino acids

Benefits: BCAAs help you build muscle and decrease soreness and, let's be honest, they make the water taste so good! The best time to have BCAAs is mixed in your water while you're working out.

Recommended brand: Xtend Natural Zero

CHIA SEEDS

What is it? These are tiny black seeds from the plant *Salvia hispanica*, which is in the same family as mint.

Benefits: Great source of omega-3 fatty acids, fiber, calcium, and phosphorus.

POWDERED PEANUT BUTTER

What is it? Peanut butter with the oil and fat content extracted.

Benefits: Good source of fiber and protein, which helps regulate your appetite. The biggest win for me on this one is it's way less messy than regular peanut butter.

Recommended brand: Naked PB

TURMERIC *(fresh root or powder)*

What is it? Turmeric, a relative to ginger, is the root from the turmeric plant, also known as *Curcuma longa*. It mainly grows in Asia and Central America, but you can grow it in your backyard as well, depending on where you live. You can get turmeric in root or powder form.

Benefits: Curcumin is the main active ingredient in turmeric. It's a powerful anti-inflammatory and antioxidant. It's said to help with chronic inflammation.

Tips: Himalayan salt and piperine (see next page) help activate the benefits of turmeric. You will see that I add these when using turmeric to activate benefits.

PIPERINE

What is it? Piperine is a bioactive compound in black pepper. It's an alkaloid like capsaicin, the active component found in chili powder and cayenne pepper.

Benefits: It boosts the absorption of curcumin, which is found in turmeric. Piperine is shown to help relieve nausea, headaches, and poor digestion.

MACA POWDER

What is it? Maca is a plant, *Lepidium meyenii*, that grows mainly in Peru. It's a cruciferous vegetable, so it's related to broccoli, cauliflower, and kale. Most of the time the root is ground into a powder before being eaten.

Benefits: It's high in vitamin C, copper, and iron. It's known to increase libido, help increase fertility in men, and also to improve mood.

MATCHA POWDER

What is it? It's a form of green tea, made from young tea leaves that are ground into a bright green powder. It's grown in the shade, which gives it higher chlorophyll levels, giving it that bright green color. Matcha is mainly grown in Japan.

Benefits: It's loaded with antioxidants and helps give you a boost of energy. It has about as much caffeine as a cup of coffee but gives you more of a relaxed feel.

COCONUT BUTTER

What is it? Coconut product made from the meat of the coconut.

Benefits: Rich in fiber, as well as iron. Boosts metabolism and can aid in weight loss.

MCT OIL

What is it? MCT oil contains medium-length chains of fats called triglycerides. It's mostly extracted from coconut oil.

Benefits: It's said to help with weight loss, promote brain health, and help protect your heart. If you have high cholesterol, you should avoid this.

GOJI BERRIES

What is it? These are little red berries that grow on shrubs known as *Lycium barbarum*. They're mainly grown in Asia.

Benefits: They're packed with antioxidants, fiber, and vitamins A and C. They're said to help with anti-aging and eye health, and they're an anti-inflammatory.

HEMP SEEDS

What is it? These are the seeds of the hemp plant, *Cannabis sativa*. They're technically considered a nut, and even though they come from the same plant as marijuana, they do not contain THC.

Benefits: They're rich in omega-3 and omega-6 fatty acids and are also great sources of protein and vitamin E.

FLAXSEEDS

What is it? Flaxseeds come from the flax plant, *Linum usitatissimum*. The plant was likely first grown in Egypt back in 3000 BC. We're still eating them today!

Benefits: They're high in protein and fiber. They're also high in omega-3 fatty acids, and so may help to lower blood pressure and cholesterol.

CACAO POWDER

What is it? Cacao powder comes from the cacao tree, *Theobroma cacao*. The tree grows large pods that contain beans. The cacao powder comes from cold pressing these beans, which removes the fat and cacao butter but retains the enzymes.

Benefits: Cacao powder is very rich in polyphenols, which are naturally occurring antioxidants. It's a major anti-inflammatory and is thought to help with blood flow to your brain and brain function.

BEE POLLEN

What is it? Bee pollen is the pollen collected by honeybees and brought back to the hive to be stored and used for food for the bees. It's a mixture of flower pollen, bee saliva, nectar, and honey.

Benefits: It's said to relieve inflammation, strengthen the immune system, reduce stress, and speed up healing.

HONEY

What is it? A thick liquid made by honeybees using the nectar of flowers; it's stored in the hive for eating during times of need.

Benefits: It's loaded with antioxidants, helps with digestive issues; it contains antifungal and antibacterial properties and can help soothe a sore throat.

Recommended brand: Local, raw honey.

CELERY JUICE

What is it? The juice of celery stalks - no leaves.

Benefits: Helps with digestion, skin, and strengthening bones. It's high in vitamin K and calcium. It's best to drink first thing in the morning on an empty stomach and wait 30 minutes before eating. You should juice the celery right before you're about to drink it. It is best within the first 60 seconds. Using a cold press juicer is best but not necessary.

BREAKFAST

Protein Smoothies

Smoothies are my go-to morning meal. They're quick and easy and they keep me powering through the day. These smoothies are packed with protein and nutrients. You can make them for your kids (or your husband), and they will never know how healthy they are.

I always buy fresh greens, strawberries, and bananas to freeze myself. You know you're getting a high-quality product, and a lot of the time it ends up being cheaper. Some of these smoothies have a lot of ingredients. I set out all of the ingredients in labeled glass containers next to the blender for easy scooping. You can combine them all into one big container and scoop out of that, but I prefer to do it individually so I know I am getting exactly what I want in each smoothie, and I can change up the recipe if I want to.

I use powdered peanut butter in place of regular peanut butter to avoid the mess. Using a NutriBullet saves time on dishes (I drink out of the same cup I blend in), and it doesn't take up much space on the counter. It's also very easy to clean, and the cup is dishwasher safe. Silicone or glass smoothies straws are a great thing to have on hand. They have wide holes that are perfect for thicker drinks, and they're dishwasher friendly.

BLUEBERRY-PEANUT BUTTER SMOOTHIE

SERVES: 1 // TOTAL TIME: 5 minutes

I use whatever greens I have on hand. When the garden is going crazy with Swiss chard, I use that. Sometimes I use kale, but spinach tastes the best. Freeze your own fresh spinach, or greens. It's higher quality than the frozen spinach you buy. Freezing helps make the smoothie really creamy, and the spinach stays good for way longer.

2 cups frozen spinach or greens of your choice

1 cup frozen blueberries

2 cups cashew milk (pg. 193) or nut milk of choice

2 scoops unflavored collagen protein powder (Bulletproof)

2 Tablespoons powdered (Naked PB) or organic peanut butter

½ teaspoon maca powder

½ teaspoon chia seeds

½ teaspoon flax seeds

½ teaspoon cacao powder

½ teaspoon matcha powder

Place all of the ingredients in a blender, and blend on high until well combined, usually about 10 seconds. If you would like a thinner consistency, just add a little more nut milk.

Tip: Adding the milk in before the powders helps it blend without powder getting stuck to the sides.

STRAWBERRY-BANANA SMOOTHIE

SERVES: 1 // TOTAL TIME: 5 minutes

Buy fresh spinach, strawberries, and bananas to pop in the freezer (make sure to wash and cut the tops off the strawberries and peel and slice the bananas prior). Freezing the spinach and the strawberries makes the smoothie super creamy and milkshake-like without having to use ice, and the fruit stays good for a long time.

1 cup frozen spinach or greens of your choice

1 frozen banana

½ cup frozen strawberries

2 cups cashew milk (pg. 193) or nut milk of choice

2 Tablespoons powdered (Naked PB) or organic peanut butter

2 scoops unflavored collagen protein powder (Bulletproof)

Place all of the ingredients in a blender, and blend on high until well combined, usually about 10 seconds. If you would like a thinner consistency, add more nut milk.

Tip: Adding the milk in before the powders helps it blend without powder getting stuck to the sides.

CHUNKY MONKEY SMOOTHIE

SERVES: 1 // TOTAL TIME: 5 minutes

Buy fresh bananas and pop them in the freezer. Make sure to peel and slice them prior. Freezing the bananas makes the smoothie super creamy and milkshake-like without having to use ice, and they stay good for a long time.

1 frozen banana

1 ½ cups cashew milk (pg. 193) or nut milk of choice

2 Tablespoons powdered (Naked PB) or organic peanut butter

1 Tablespoon cacao powder

2 scoops unflavored collagen protein powder (Bulletproof)

Place all the ingredients in a blender, and blend on high until well combined, usually about 10 seconds. If you would like a thinner consistency, add more nut milk.

Tip: Adding the milk in before the powders helps it blend without powder getting stuck to the sides.

COCONUT YOGURT BOWL

SERVES: 1 // TOTAL TIME: 10 minutes

I used to eat Greek yogurt with fruit and granola every morning. Once dairy was cut out of my diet, I needed to find a substitute, and coconut yogurt does the trick. This bowl is loaded with healthy fruits, nuts, seeds, and protein. It can be enjoyed for breakfast, a snack, or even dessert. The kids love it too! I recommend using plain coconut yogurt. The flavored yogurts contain a lot of sugar, and you can get that same awesome flavor kick by adding all-natural ingredients. It's light, refreshing, and packed with protein. The options here are endless— you can add so many different things to the bowl to customize it to your liking.

6 oz plain coconut yogurt

1-2 scoops unflavored collagen protein powder (Bulletproof)

½ cup sliced fresh strawberries

¼ cup fresh blueberries

¼ cup granola (Kind Vanilla-Blueberry)

½ teaspoon chia seeds

½ teaspoon flax seeds

1 teaspoon dried goji berries

1 Tablespoon local, raw honey

2 Tablespoons raw walnuts, raw almonds, or any other raw nut of choice

1 teaspoon coconut shavings

1. In a bowl, mix the yogurt and protein powder together until well combined.

2. Add the fruit, granola, seeds, and goji berries.

3. Top with honey, nuts, and coconut shavings.

Tip: I love going to the farmers market and purchasing my yogurt there. If your farmers market carries it, I recommend buying it! But if not, you can find it at most grocery stores. So Delicious is my favorite store bought brand.

AVOCADO TOAST

SERVES: 2 // TOTAL TIME: 15 minutes

Avocado toast took off at trendy brunch places not too long ago. And why wouldn't it? Not only is it ridiculously tasty, it's also beautiful. This is one of the first breakfast meals I started making when I met my husband, and it impressed him. This recipe is easy, and I really love all of these flavors together.

Tip: If you cook eggs often, I highly recommend getting an Egg Central on Amazon. It makes perfect poached or hard-boiled eggs with just the flick of a switch.

2 slices gluten-free bread

1 Tablespoon Kerrygold butter or dairy-free butter, at room temperature

2 eggs

1 firm, ripe avocado, peeled and pitted

½ teaspoon garlic salt

Juice of 1 lemon

1 cup arugula or micro greens

½ cup cherry tomatoes, sliced

1 clove garlic, sliced

1 teaspoon balsamic reduction

Flaky sea salt and freshly ground black pepper, to taste

1. Toast the bread to your desired toastiness, and spread the butter evenly over both pieces.

2. Poach your eggs: Bring a pot of water to a simmer, stir to create a whirlpool, carefully pour one egg into the center and cook for 3 minutes; remove with a slotted spoon. Repeat with the other egg. Or use an Egg Central on the poach setting.

3. In a small bowl, mash the avocado to your desired chunkiness and add the garlic salt and lemon juice. Mix well and set aside.

4. When the toast is finished, spread the avocado on the toast thick enough so you can't see the bread. Sprinkle on the arugula, then add the poached egg.

5. Add the cherry tomatoes and garlic, and top with a drizzle of balsamic reduction. Sprinkle salt and pepper on top.

BLUEBERRY PROTEIN MUFFINS

MAKES: 15 muffins // TOTAL TIME: 20 minutes

Talk about yum! These blueberry muffins are to die for. They're very simple to make, and they're great to have on hand as a snack or a breakfast on the go. These gooey, yummy, protein-packed muffins contain no flour of any sort. You can use store-bought cashew butter, but I like to make my own. It's so simple and much cheaper than buying it at the store. You can find the recipe for nut butters on pg. 196.

Avocado oil cooking spray

1 ¾ cups cashew butter (pg. 196)

½ cup coconut sugar

2 eggs

½ teaspoon vanilla extract

½ teaspoon baking soda

½ teaspoon coarse sea salt

2 scoops unflavored collagen protein powder (Bulletproof)

⅔ cup fresh blueberries

1. Preheat the oven to 350°F, and spray a silicone muffin tray with cooking spray.

2. In a stand mixer, mix together the cashew butter, sugar, eggs, and vanilla. Add in the baking soda, salt, and protein powder. Mix until well combined.

3. Fold in the blueberries with a silicone spatula, being careful not to burst any of them. The dough will be pretty sticky.

4. Spoon the dough into the muffin tray, filling it to the top. Bake for 8–10 minutes, or until a toothpick poked in the center comes out clean.

5. Remove from the oven and let cool before popping out the muffins to enjoy. Will keep in an airtight container at room temperature for 2 days or up to 5 days in the fridge.

CRISPY HASH BROWNS

SERVES: 4 // TOTAL TIME: 30 minutes

This hash browns recipe makes the kids go crazy; they ask me to make them every morning. They're made with just a few ingredients and are way healthier than any hash browns you will ever buy frozen or at a restaurant. If you have a griddle, that is the perfect way to cook them, but you can also use a skillet or two.

Tip: Your food processor has a shred disk attachment that sits at the top of the processor bowl. Use this to shred the potatoes. It's a huge time-saver. If you don't have the attachment, a hand shredder will work just fine.

2 Tablespoons Kerrygold butter, dairy-free butter, or coconut oil

2 russet potatoes, peeled

½ cup cassava flour

1 egg

1 teaspoon Himalayan salt

1 teaspoon freshly ground pepper

Ketchup, for serving

1. If you have a griddle, turn the heat to 400°F and let heat up. If you're using a skillet, you will need two; heat them over medium heat.

2. Shred the potato either in the food processor or by hand.

3. Immerse the shredded potatoes in cold water, and strain; repeat 2–3 times or as many times as it takes for the water to run clear. Use a nut bag or your hands to wring the water out of the potatoes. Spread them on a paper towel and pat them dry.

4. Place the shredded potatoes, cassava flour, egg, salt, and pepper in a large bowl. Mix with your hands until well combined.

5. Once hot, melt the butter or coconut oil on the griddle or skillets. If using a griddle, spread the potatoes evenly over the griddle, about a ½-inch-thick layer, using a spatula to pat them down so they're even. If you're using two skillets, split them up evenly between the two and use a spatula to pat them down even. Let cook until golden brown, about 8–10 minutes. Cut into quarters, and flip over to cook the other side for another 8 minutes, or until golden brown.

6. Serve immediately with ketchup.

OVERNIGHT OATS

SERVES: 1 // TOTAL TIME: 5 minutes

Ever run out the front door without breakfast because you're too rushed to cook? If so, this recipe is for you. These overnight oats are quick and easy. You make them the night before and store them in the fridge. It's an easy grab-and-go meal in the morning on your way to work. It's packed with protein and nutrients to help you power through the day.

1 cup gluten-free rolled oats

1 scoop unflavored collagen protein powder (Bulletproof)

1 cup almond milk (pg. 192) or nut milk of choice

1 Tablespoon vanilla extract

1 Tablespoon chia seeds

1 Tablespoon maple syrup

Fresh fruit, for topping

Local, raw honey, for topping

1. Combine oats, protein powder, milk, vanilla, chia seeds, and syrup in a Mason jar and stir to combine. Put on the lid and let sit in the fridge overnight.

2. In the morning, either heat it up on the stove over medium heat or eat it cold. Top it with fresh fruit of your choice and a drizzle of honey.

CHIA PUDDING

SERVES: 1 // TOTAL TIME: 5 minutes

A breakfast that makes itself overnight in the fridge? Yes please! I love making chia pudding. It's super easy and can be kept in a Mason jar for easy grab-and-go in the morning or for a snack during the day. Top with any fruit, nuts, or seeds you like!

2 Tablespoons chia seeds

½ cup cashew milk (pg. 193) or nut milk of choice

1 teaspoon local, raw honey, plus more for topping

2 scoops unflavored collagen protein powder (Bulletproof)

Fresh fruit, for topping (optional)

Raw nuts or seeds, for topping (optional)

1. Pour chia seeds, milk, honey, and protein powder into a Mason jar and shake well. Let settle for 2 minutes and shake again.

2. Make sure the lid is on tight and place in the fridge to set for at least 2 hours.

3. When you're ready to eat, top with fruit, honey, nuts, or whatever else you'd like.

PROTEIN PANCAKES

MAKES: 8 pancakes // TOTAL TIME: 20 minutes

I gave up on pancakes a long time ago because they were always so difficult to make correctly. Mine always turned out deformed and burnt, but this recipe has restored my faith! These protein-packed pancakes are really easy to make. They're delicious, and you would never know they're gluten-free. This is a go-to for my husband when he is making breakfast for the kids. He has now mastered the pancake-making in our household, and the kids do not let me make them anymore. He loves to make one huge pancake to impress the kids on Sunday mornings.

Tip: Make sure to let the batter set for 8 minutes; it thickens, making them easier to flip.

2 eggs

¼ cup cashew milk (pg. 193) or nut milk of choice

2 Tablespoons maple syrup, plus more for serving

½ cup unsweetened applesauce

1 ½ cups gluten-free rolled oats

2–4 scoops unflavored collagen protein powder (Bulletproof)

2 teaspoons baking powder

½ teaspoon vanilla extract

Kerrygold butter or dairy-free butter at room temperature, for pan and serving

Fresh fruit, for serving

1. Place eggs, milk, syrup, applesauce, oats, 2 scoops protein powder (add more for an extra protein boost if you like), baking powder, and vanilla into a food processor or blender. Blend on high for about 1 minute, or until well combined. Allow the pancake batter to sit for 8 minutes to thicken.

2. Heat a griddle or nonstick skillet over medium heat. Once it's hot, lightly grease the surface with butter, and pour ¼ cup batter for each pancake. Make sure to give yourself enough space between each pancake to flip. Allow the pancakes to cook until they start to bubble and the edges are set, about 45 seconds to 1 minute. With a wide, flat spatula (I like to use metal), flip the pancakes and let them cook on the other side until golden brown, another 30 seconds or so. Repeat with the rest of the batter.

3. Top with butter, fresh fruit, and maple syrup.

SALADS

BUTTERNUT SALAD // 54

WATERMELON SALAD // 56

BEET SALAD // 58

JICAMA SALAD // 60

CUCUMBER SALAD // 63

EGG SALAD // 64

MIMI'S THAI STEAK SALAD // 66

TRICOLOR PEAR & ARUGULA SALAD // 69

HEART OF PALM SALAD // 70

BUTTERNUT SALAD

SERVES: 4 // TOTAL TIME: 25 minutes

One year we had a butternut squash plant that popped up out of nowhere in our garden. Next thing you know, we had this huge vine that covered a ton of ground and produced over forty butternuts that season. We had such a surplus, and I was trying to make just about anything with them so they wouldn't go to waste. I would never have thought to put butternut squash in a salad, but it's delicious. This salad is super refreshing, and you can top with any protein you like.

Salad

½ small butternut squash

Avocado oil cooking spray

Himalayan salt and freshly ground pepper, to taste

1 head romaine lettuce, chopped

½ cup cherry tomatoes, sliced

½ cup marinated artichoke hearts, chopped

½ white onion, sliced

2 Tablespoons raw sliced almonds

Champagne Vinaigrette

½ cup avocado or grapeseed oil

¼ cup champagne or white wine vinegar

Juice of ½ lemon

1 Tablespoon Dijon mustard

1 Tablespoon local, raw honey

3 cloves garlic, minced

1 teaspoon cracked red pepper

1. Peel the butternut squash; scoop out and discard the stringy center in your compost bin or trash can. Slice the squash into thin strips.

2. Heat a large skillet over medium-high heat, and spray with cooking spray. Add the butternut slices. Sprinkle lightly with salt and pepper and cook, stirring occasionally, for about 6–8 minutes, or until tender.

3. In a large serving bowl, place the lettuce, tomatoes, artichoke hearts, onions and cooked butternut squash.

4. In a small bowl, whisk together all of the ingredients for the dressing until well combined. Pour a quarter of the dressing over the salad and toss to combine. Top with sliced almonds. Place the remaining dressing on the table for serving.

WATERMELON SALAD

SERVES: 2 // TOTAL TIME: 10 minutes

When I was little, I would eat watermelon with salt at my grandparents' house. I've always loved watermelon, and it makes me think of summer, my all-time favorite season. My dad loves watermelon, too. When I go to his house, still to this day, he often has a huge watermelon sliced in half with a spoon in it sitting in the fridge. When he gets hungry, he goes and grabs the watermelon and spoons it into his mouth straight from the rind. No dishes necessary. This watermelon salad is delicious. It adds a perfect sweet crunch and is great for a summer day.

Salad

2 cups spinach

1 cup arugula

4 cups cubed watermelon

¼ red onion, thinly sliced

½ cup cherry tomatoes, sliced

½ cucumber, peeled and sliced into half moons

1 firm, ripe avocado, peeled, pitted and cubed

Handful of raw pumpkin seeds

Handful of raw walnuts

Sprinkle of dried goji berries

Himalayan salt and freshly ground black pepper, to taste

Watermelon Vinaigrette

2 cups cubed watermelon

¼ cup local, raw honey

1 Tablespoon apple cider vinegar

1 Tablespoon Dijon mustard

1 teaspoon Himalayan salt

½ cup avocado or grapeseed oil

1. In a large bowl, place the spinach, arugula, watermelon, onion, cherry tomatoes, cucumber, and avocado. Gently toss to combine. Lightly salt and pepper the salad.

2. To make the dressing, place the watermelon, honey, apple cider vinegar, Dijon mustard, and salt into a food processor or blender. Blend on high until well combined and smooth. Turn to low, and slowly add in the avocado or grapeseed oil, blending until emulsified.

3. Drizzle ¼ cup of the dressing over the top of the salad and toss lightly to coat. Top with pumpkin seeds, walnuts, and goji berries. Place the remaining dressing on the table for serving.

BEET SALAD

SERVES: 2 // TOTAL TIME: 40 minutes

When I was living in Austin, I used to frequent Vinaigrette, this amazing salad restaurant. Every time I went, I always ordered the beet salad; it never changed. It is so delicious. When I moved to California, I missed being able to go grab this at lunchtime. So I created my own recipe to fill my void. You can preboil the beets, quarter them, and store them in the fridge to save time. When you're ready to make the salad, just throw them in cold and you're ready to go. You can also add grilled chicken or shrimp for an extra protein boost.

Tip: Use yellow beets and avoid the mess of the red beets.

Salad

4 large beets (yellow or red)

1 cup chopped romaine lettuce

2 cups spinach leaves

½ cup cherry tomatoes, sliced

¼ white onion, sliced

¼ cup pistachios

1 Tablespoon hemp seeds

¼ cup crumbled goat cheese (optional)

Grilled chicken or shrimp (optional)

Champagne Vinaigrette

½ cup avocado or grapeseed oil

¼ cup champagne or white wine vinegar

Juice of ½ lemon

1 Tablespoon Dijon mustard

1 Tablespoon local, raw honey

3 cloves garlic, minced

1 teaspoon cracked red pepper

1. Boil the beets in a pot of water for 25 minutes, or until cooked through but still firm and the skins peel off easily. Run them under cold water and peel off the skins. Cut beets into quarters and set aside to cool.

2. Meanwhile, in a large bowl, combine romaine, spinach, tomatoes, onions, and beets. Add the chicken or shrimp, if using.

3. To make the dressing, combine all of the ingredients in a small glass bowl and whisk until well combined.

4. Pour half of the dressing over the salad and lightly toss. Top with pistachios, hemp seeds, and goat cheese, if using. Place the remaining dressing on the table for serving.

JICAMA SALAD

SERVES: 4 // TOTAL TIME: 25 minutes

I don't even know where to start with this salad. It's ahhh-mazing. I end up licking the bowl clean, because there is no way I am going to waste even the tiniest bit of the delicious mint cream. I had this salad at one of my favorite restaurants in Tulum and haven't been able to stop making it since. I had to put a couple twists on the recipe to make it dairy-free, but it's even more delicious this way; we ordered it recently when we were visiting, and we liked my version even better than theirs.

Tips: To supreme an orange: Use a sharp knife to slice off the tops and bottoms of each orange. Following the curve of each orange with your knife, slice off all of the skin, including the white pith. Cut out the segments from the membranes.

Use a mandoline slicer for the jicama to make the slicing process go faster.

Salad

1 large jicama, peeled and sliced thin

3 oranges, supremed

Handful of mint leaves

½ cup raw pumpkin seeds, toasted in a dry skillet until lightly browned, for serving

Honey-Lime Marinade

¼ cup freshly squeezed orange juice

½ cup avocado or grapeseed oil

2 Tablespoons local, raw honey

1 teaspoon flaky sea salt

Mint Cream

1 Tablespoon raw pumpkin seeds, toasted in a dry skillet until lightly browned

1 cup loosely packed mint leaves

½ cup avocado or grapeseed oil

1 Tablespoon local, raw honey

¼ cup fresh squeezed orange juice

1 cup Tofutti milk-free sour cream

1 teaspoon flaky sea salt

1. Combine the jicama, oranges, and mint in a large bowl.

2. In a small bowl, whisk together all of the ingredients for the honey-lime marinade. Pour over the jicama and toss to coat.

3. To make the mint cream, combine all of the ingredients in a food processor or blender. Blend on high for 30 seconds or until well combined, scraping down the sides as necessary. The consistency should be creamy and thick.

4. Coat the bottom of each serving bowl with a generous amount of the mint cream, pile the jicama salad on top, and sprinkle with toasted pumpkin seeds.

CUCUMBER SALAD

SERVES: 2 // TOTAL TIME: 10 minutes

This is a fun salad that's full of fresh veggies and flavor. It's a very quick fix and can be served as a salad or a side dish. I love to slice the garlic thick so that you get a nice flavor burst, but you can slice it thin or mince it if you like. I cut up the cucumber without seeding it, but if you wish to seed then slice, go for it. You can also bulk this dish up with some grilled shrimp. Yum!

Salad

3 cups cherry tomatoes, quartered

¼ red onion, sliced

2 firm, ripe avocados, peeled, pitted and cubed

3 cloves garlic, sliced

1 cucumber, peeled and sliced into half-moons

Champagne Vinaigrette

½ cup avocado or grapeseed oil

¼ cup champagne or white wine vinegar

Juice of ½ lemon

1 Tablespoon Dijon mustard

1 Tablespoon local, raw honey

3 cloves garlic, minced

1 teaspoon cracked red pepper

Combine all of the ingredients for the salad in a large bowl. In a separate small bowl, whisk together the dressing ingredients until well combined. Pour the dressing over the top of the salad and use a spoon to lightly toss, being careful to not mush the avocado.

EGG SALAD

SERVES: 4 // TOTAL TIME: 20 minutes

This is a little spin on the Southern deviled egg. At every family holiday gathering, we always have dozens of deviled eggs. Several people bring them, and everyone makes them just a little differently—all amazing. My dad can eat an entire dozen in one sitting, and one of my favorite things to do is video him plowing them down. I swear he doesn't chew!

Making deviled eggs can be a bit tedious, trying for the perfect peeling and slicing of the eggs. But this egg salad takes that tedious part away, as it doesn't matter how the egg looks. You mix everything together and serve it as a salad or a wrap on a romaine lettuce leaf. I added a fun little twist with lemon and dill to make this even more flavorful.

¼ cup mayonnaise

2 Tablespoons Dijon mustard

2 Tablespoons chopped fresh dill

1 Tablespoon freshly squeezed lemon juice

½ teaspoon Himalayan salt

½ teaspoon freshly ground black pepper

½ teaspoon paprika

8 hard-boiled eggs, peeled and chopped

½ white onion, chopped

2-3 large celery stalks, chopped

20 firm green or purple grapes, sliced

6 whole romaine leaves, for serving (optional)

In a small bowl, whisk together the mayonnaise, Dijon, dill, lemon juice, salt, pepper, and paprika. Place the chopped eggs in a large bowl and add the mayonnaise mixture; mix lightly to coat. Fold in the onions, celery, and grapes. Serve immediately, or store in the fridge in an airtight container for up to 3 days.

Tip: If you cook eggs often, I highly recommend getting an Egg Central on Amazon. It makes perfect poached or hard-boiled eggs with just the flick of a switch.

MIMI'S THAI STEAK SALAD

SERVES: 4 // TOTAL TIME: 40 minutes

Mimi (or Debbie), my mom, is obsessed with this salad. She got the idea from Bartlett's, one of her favorite restaurants in Austin. We would always go there when she came to visit me in Austin. One day when she was visiting me in California, we recreated it, and damn, was it good. You can switch the steak for chicken or shrimp, or ditch it altogether and make it a vegetarian salad. Using fresh, gluten-free noodles is a game changer. I buy them in the refrigerator section at the grocery store, but they can also be found at your local farmers market.

Salad

1 lb filet mignon (my preference), or other steak of choice

1 Tablespoon olive oil

½ teaspoon Himalayan salt

¼ teaspoon freshly ground black pepper

9 oz gluten-free linguini noodles (Taste Republic)

1 cup spinach leaves

1 cup thinly sliced red or napa cabbage

1 cup loosely packed basil

1 cup loosely packed cilantro

1 cup loosely packed mint

1 cucumber, peeled and thinly sliced into half moons

¼ cup chopped scallions, for serving

1 firm, ripe avocado, peeled, pitted and cubed

¼ cup raw cashews, for serving (optional)

Dressing

⅓ cup freshly squeezed lime juice

Grated zest of 1 lime

¼ cup local, raw honey

1 Tablespoon grated fresh ginger

1 Tablespoon chili paste (optional)

1 Tablespoon fish sauce

½ cup tamari

¼ cup avocado or grapeseed oil

1. Make the dressing: In a small bowl, whisk together all of the ingredients for the dressing until well combined. Set aside.

2. Rub the steak with a little olive oil and season with salt and pepper. Put it into a gallon resealable bag and spoon a quarter of the dressing into the bag. Let the steak marinate in the dressing for 15 minutes.

3. Grease the grill grate or grill pan and heat it to 450°F. Grill the steak to the desired doneness, but for this salad medium-rare is best. For medium-rare, cook the steak on direct heat for 3 minutes on each side, then cook on indirect heat for 3 minutes each side. If you would like it more well-done, keep it on a few extra minutes. Once the steak is done, let it sit for 5 minutes before slicing it thin, against the grain.

4. Meanwhile, cook the noodles according to the package directions. Rinse with cold water and set aside.

5. Place the spinach, cabbage, basil, cilantro, mint, cucumber, and noodles in a large bowl, and toss with the remaining dressing. Divide the salad among four plates and top with steak, scallions, avocado, and cashews, if using.

TRICOLOR PEAR & ARUGULA SALAD

SERVES: 4 // TOTAL TIME: 15 minutes

This salad is almost too beautiful to eat. I love the color pop of the pears and craisins. If you don't like pears, you can always swap out for apples. You can also add grilled chicken or shrimp for more protein. This salad is best served in a glass bowl to show off all of the layers.

Salad

4 cups baby arugula

½ firm, ripe red pear

½ firm, ripe green pear

½ firm, ripe brown pear

½ cup raw walnuts

½ cup craisins

¼ white onion, thinly sliced

Himalayan salt and freshly ground black pepper, to taste

¼ cup crumbled goat cheese (optional)

Dressing

⅓ cup avocado or grapeseed oil

¼ cup champagne vinegar

3 cloves garlic, minced

1 teaspoon Dijon mustard

2 Tablespoons freshly squeezed orange juice

½ teaspoon garlic salt

1 Tablespoon local, raw honey

1. Make the dressing: In a small bowl, combine all of the dressing ingredients and whisk until well combined. Set aside.

2. Spread half of the arugula in the bottom of a large glass serving bowl. Arrange a layer of the red pears on top of the arugula, skins facing outwards. Add in half of the walnuts, craisins, and onions; sprinkle with salt and pepper. Repeat the layers with green pears then brown pears until you reach the top.

3. Pour ¼ cup of the dressing over the top and sprinkle with goat cheese, if using. Place the remaining dressing on the table for serving.

HEART OF PALM SALAD

SERVES: 4 // TOTAL TIME: 5 minutes

I make this dish several times a week. It's so simple, yet so delicious. It takes less than ten minutes to make and does really well stored in the fridge. This makes a delicious salad, side, or snack. I recommend the hearts of palm that come in glass jars. They're better quality than the cans (sometimes the cans have some hearts that are too hard to consume).

Tip: To julienne basil, stack the leaves, roll them up like a cigar, and slice. This helps keep the oils intact and saves the flavor.

2 (14.5-oz) jars hearts of palm, drained and chopped into ½-inch pieces

5 large basil leaves, julienned

3–4 Tablespoons avocado or grapeseed oil

½ cup raw pecans, chopped

½ teaspoon garlic salt

Combine all of the ingredients into a large bowl and mix together with a spoon. Serve immediately or store in the fridge for later.

APPETIZERS

MEATBALLS WITH TOMATO SAUCE

SERVES: 4 // TOTAL TIME: 30 minutes

These meatballs are really easy to whip up, and they're so tasty. They're the perfect appetizer for a party, addition to your spaghetti, or topper for your yummy gluten-free sub. Any way you eat them, they will not disappoint. Nutritional yeast is a dairy-free option that adds cheesy flavor without the stomachache.

1 lb grass-fed ground beef

1 lb ground pork

½ cup gluten-free panko bread crumbs

1 egg

4 cloves garlic, minced

2 Tablespoons shallots, chopped

1 teaspoon ground cumin

1 teaspoon onion powder

1 teaspoon garlic salt

1 teaspoon cracked red pepper

1 Tablespoon curry powder

Nutritional yeast, for serving

Basil, for garnish

Sauce

1 (28-oz) can crushed tomatoes

1 (15-oz) can tomato sauce

1 Tablespoon brown sugar

1 Tablespoon Worcestershire sauce

3 Tablespoons Italian seasoning

1 teaspoon onion powder

1 teaspoon celery salt

1 teaspoon garlic salt

3 cloves garlic, minced

1. Preheat the oven to 400°F and line a rimmed baking sheet with reusable parchment paper.

2. In a large bowl, combine all of the ingredients for the meatballs and mix well with your hands. Roll into 2-inch balls and transfer to the baking sheet. Bake for 15–18 minutes, or until they're cooked through.

3. Meanwhile, place all of the ingredients for the sauce in a large pot. Bring to a slight boil, reduce the heat, cover, and let simmer until the meatballs are ready.

4. Spoon the sauce over the meatballs, top with nutritional yeast, and garnish with basil. You can use gluten-free noodles or spaghetti squash to make spaghetti and meatballs.

THAI MUSSELS

SERVES: 4-6 // TOTAL TIME: 40 minutes

Did you know that cooking a delicious bowl of mussels only takes about ten minutes? The most time-consuming part is cleaning and debearding the mussels, but it's worth it. I use a spoon to help scrape off all of the gunk on the shell while running cold water over it. If you have a local fish market near you, that's the best place to buy fresh mussels, and some markets sell them already cleaned. On the weekends, Costco has a great seafood setup as well.

3 lb fresh mussels, cleaned and debearded

1 (13.5-oz) can full-fat coconut milk

⅓ cup freshly squeezed lime juice

Grated zest of 1 lime

⅓ cup dry white wine

1 Tablespoon fish sauce

1 Tablespoon coconut sugar

2 Tablespoons curry powder

3 serrano peppers, sliced thin

1 (4-oz) jar green curry paste

5 cloves garlic, minced

¼ cup chopped fresh cilantro, for garnish

1. Clean and debeard the mussels thoroughly. Throw out any that are cracked or not closed all the way. Rinse them one more time to make sure they're all clean and ready to go. Set aside in a bowl.

2. In a large stockpot, bring coconut milk, lime juice, lime zest, wine, fish sauce, coconut sugar, curry powder, serranos, curry paste, and garlic to a boil over high heat.

3. Reduce the heat to medium, and carefully stir in the mussels. Cover and cook for 5–8 minutes, stirring occasionally. Throw out any mussels that did not open.

4. Top with fresh cilantro and serve immediately.

CRAB CAKES

MAKES: 6 // TOTAL TIME: 25 minutes

Growing up with parents who are not big fish eaters, I was never introduced to fresh fish. At home we would eat canned tuna or shrimp cocktail, but that was about all I had tried before I went to college. From college on, I began to branch out and started eating the good stuff, and it wasn't until my late 20s that I ever tried a crab cake. For years, I was intimidated to try to make these at home, because they seemed difficult. One day I gave it a go and was surprised at how easy it was. Now I love making them. They're a great appetizer, snack, or even main course.

Crab Cakes

Avocado oil cooking spray

⅓ cup mayonnaise

1 large egg

2 Tablespoons Dijon mustard

1 Tablespoon Worcestershire sauce

1 Tablespoon sriracha (optional)

⅛ teaspoon Himalayan salt

⅛ teaspoon freshly ground black pepper

1 lb wild-caught jumbo lump crabmeat

1 cup gluten-free panko bread crumbs

Avocado oil, for frying

Lemon wedges, for serving

Sauce

½ cup mayonnaise

3 Tablespoons Dijon mustard

⅛ teaspoon garlic salt

1 teaspoon onion powder

1 teaspoon cayenne pepper

1 Tablespoon capers

1. Spray a large skillet or griddle with cooking spray and place over medium heat. In a small bowl, whisk together mayo, egg, mustard, Worcestershire sauce, sriracha, salt, and pepper. Set aside.

2. In a blender or food processor, blend the panko until powdered. In a medium bowl, mix together crabmeat and ½ cup of the powdered panko. Fold in the mayo mixture and form into patties (should make 5–7 patties, depending on size).

3. Put the other ½ cup powdered panko into a shallow, wide bowl, and dredge each crab cake in it to fully coat. Drizzle a little avocado oil on both sides of each cake, and place them on the hot griddle or skillet, leaving enough room to flip. Cook until golden and crispy, 4–5 minutes per side.

4. While the crab cakes are cooking, make the sauce. Combine all of the ingredients in a blender or food processor and blend on high until smooth; add more cayenne if you want the extra kick. Spoon into a bowl.

5. Serve crab cakes immediately with sauce on the side.

ARTICHOKE & BUTTER SAUCE

SERVES: 1-2 // TOTAL TIME: 45 minutes

I used to eat artichokes with lemon-butter sauce all the time when I was little. I remember always scarfing down the leaves so I could get to the heart. Letting the heart soak in the butter sauce and using a large spoon to scoop it out with a ton of sauce is the best part. My mouth is watering just thinking about it. I've continued to make these all throughout my life. Now that I am living in California, I have several artichoke plants in my backyard. I would have never guessed they grew on a large stalk with each plant producing about fifteen to twenty artichokes. I eat at least one a day when they're in season to keep up with how many the plants produce. If you let the artichoke bloom on the plant, it turns into a beautiful purple flower that lasts for weeks in a vase.

---

1 artichoke

4 Tablespoons Kerrygold butter or dairy-free butter

½ teaspoon garlic salt

Juice of 2 lemons

1. Bring 8 cups of water to a boil in a medium pot. Put the artichoke in the water and boil for 45 minutes or until the leaves are soft. You can pull off a leaf and taste it to see if it's tender and ready to eat.

2. When the artichoke is almost done, melt the butter in a small glass bowl in the microwave for 20–30 seconds. Add in the garlic salt and lemon; stir to combine.

3. Use tongs to get the artichoke out of the boiling water. Turn upside down to drain out any excess water.

4. Serve with the warm lemon-butter sauce for dipping.

PICKLE SANDWICH

SERVES: 1 // TOTAL TIME: 15 minutes

I've loved pickles since I was a kid. Giant pickles remind me of being at the softball park either in-between games or watching my sister play when we were kids. I don't know why it took me so long in life to realize I should be using pickles instead of bread for sandwiches, but better late than never. I love to make a pickle sandwich for lunch when I am in a hurry and need something quick. Boar's Head honey turkey is my all-time favorite deli meat. It has to be shaved so thin it's falling apart; I have no idea why, but this makes it taste so much better. Sweet cherry peppers can be found in the assorted olive section of the grocery store. The options are endless for what you can top them with. For a little extra spice, instead of a pickle, you can hollow out a large jalapeño and add all the toppings to make a jalapeño sandwich.

Tip: Adding jalapeño potato chips (Kettle) to the pickle sandwich adds a delicious crunch.

---

1 whole pickle (Claussen)

3 slices salami or pepperoni

1 oz shredded honey turkey (Boars Head) or meat of choice

2 sweet cherry peppers, sliced

2 tomato slices

Handful of alfalfa sprouts

Dash of champagne vinegar

Dash of avocado or grapeseed oil

Himalayan salt and freshly ground black pepper, to taste

1. Cut the pickle in half lengthwise and scoop out the middle with a spoon, so the halves look like boats.

2. In a small skillet, cook the salami or pepperoni on medium heat for 30 seconds per side. Drain on a paper towel.

3. Put the turkey, salami or pepperoni, and all other ingredients on top of one pickle half. Top with the other half and secure with a toothpick if needed.

Ceviches

Mexico is my favorite place to travel. The food is delicious, and the service is unbeatable. Every time I go, I always feel so refreshed and relaxed when returning home. I owe it to eating fresh fish every meal, getting lots of vitamin C, and swimming in salt water.

You know what Mexico is really, really great at? Ceviche! When I am in Mexico, I just can't get enough. It took me a long time to actually try to make it at home, because I was always scared of it not being cooked all the way or the fish not being super fresh. As long as you are going to your local market and getting fresh, not frozen, fish, it really is a piece of cake to make. I usually chop up the fish right after I get it and put it in a lidded glass container covered in lime juice. It can be ready to eat within a hour, or you can leave it overnight and make it for lunch the next day. I always buy wild-caught fish, because the meat is leaner and it's higher in fatty acids. You can use so many different kinds of fish, but my favorites are yellowtail, grouper, halibut, and shrimp. It's important to use only fresh lime juice; do not use any kind of bottled lime juice.

You will need to strain the blended bases for some of these ceviches. I prefer to use a nut bag; you can find them on Amazon. They're really easy to clean and work great. If you're trying to cut out corn chips, you can always sub out taro chips for serving.

Tip: To supreme an orange: Use a sharp knife to slice off the tops and bottoms of each orange. Following the curve of each orange with your knife, slice off all of the skin, including the white pith. Cut out the segments from the membranes. If you're too lazy or don't have enough time to supreme an orange, just cut it into small, thin pieces and add it into the ceviche.

COCONUT MILK CEVICHE

SERVES: 4 // TOTAL TIME: 1 hour

1 lb wild-caught white fish of choice, or sliced coconut meat (vegan)

1 cup freshly squeezed lime juice, or enough to cover the fish

2 oranges

½ (13.5-oz) can full-fat coconut milk, well shaken

1 teaspoon local, raw honey

1 tablespoon raw pumpkin seeds, for topping

¼ red onion, sliced thin

½ jicama, peeled and cut into batons

1 firm, ripe avocado, peeled, pitted and cubed

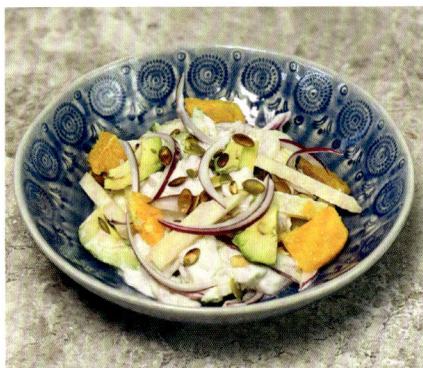

1. Rinse the fish and pat dry with a paper towel. Cut it into small chunks, the smaller the better since they're "cooking" in lime juice. Put the fish in a glass container with a lid, and cover with the lime juice. Cover, and let sit in the fridge for at least 1 hour or let sit overnight to make the next day.

2. When the fish is close to done (opaque), juice half of one orange. In a medium bowl, whisk together the coconut milk, honey, and orange juice.

3. Supreme the remaining oranges (see pg. 84).

4. In a small, dry skillet over medium-low heat, toast the pumpkin seeds, until golden browned, stirring frequently to keep from burning.

5. Using a slotted spoon, add the fish to the coconut mixture and toss until coated. If using coconut meat, toss to coat in the coconut mixture. Spoon the fish or coconut meat into serving bowls. Top with red onion slices, jicama batons, avocado, orange segments, and toasted pumpkin seeds.

AGUACHILE

SERVES: 4 // TOTAL TIME: 1 hour

½ lb wild-caught shrimp, peeled and deveined

1 ½ cups freshly squeezed lime juice

1 cup cilantro leaves, plus more for garnish

1 cucumber, sliced into half moons

½ red or white onion

1–2 large jalapeño peppers, halved

1 slice fresh pineapple, chopped (about ¼ cup)

2 cloves garlic

1 habanero pepper, sliced (optional)

1 firm, ripe avocado, peeled, pitted and cubed

1 teaspoon Himalayan salt

Tortilla or taro chips, for serving

1. Rinse the shrimp and pat dry with a paper towel. Slice the shrimp in half lengthwise and then again crosswise. Trying to not overlap, place in a large shallow glass bowl with a lid; add enough lime juice to cover the shrimp (about 1 cup). Cover, and put in the fridge for at least 1 hour or until pink, flipping halfway through. You can also let sit overnight to make the next day.

2. Meanwhile, combine the cilantro, half of the cucumber, half of the red onion, the jalapeño, pineapple, garlic, and the remaining ½ cup lime juice in a food processor or blender. Blend on high until smooth, scraping down the sides as necessary. Use a nut bag or cheesecloth to strain the base into the serving bowl; add a little of the pulp back in if desired. Discard the rest into your compost bin or trash can.

3. When the shrimp is "cooked" (mostly all pink), use a slotted spoon to transfer it to the serving bowl. Thinly slice the remainder of the red onion and chop up the remaining cucumber.

4. Add onions, habaneros (if using), cucumbers, and avocado. Lightly toss, garnish with chopped cilantro, and serve with tortilla or taro chips.

CUCUMBER-BASIL CEVICHE

SERVES: 4 // TOTAL TIME: 1 hour

1 lb wild caught grouper or white fish of choice

1 cup freshly squeezed lime juice

1 cucumber, peeled and chopped

5-6 fresh basil leaves, plus more for topping

1 jalapeño pepper

½ cup coconut water

3 oranges

½ jicama, peeled and cut into batons

¼ red onion, sliced thin

1 firm, ripe avocado, peeled, pitted and cubed

Flaky sea salt, for serving

1. Rinse the fish and pat dry with a paper towel. Cut it into small chunks, the smaller the better since they're "cooking" in lime juice. Put the fish in a glass container with a lid and cover with the lime juice. Cover and let sit in the fridge for at least 1 hour, or let sit overnight to make the next day.

2. When the fish is close to done (opaque), cut three quarters of the cucumber into chunks and place it, the basil, jalapeño, coconut water, and the juice of 1 orange in a blender or food processor. Blend on high until well combined and fully liquidized. Use a nut bag to strain the juice out into a bowl; discard the pulp into your trash can or compost bin.

3. Supreme the remaining 2 oranges (see pg. 84).

4. Place ⅓ cup of the cucumber-basil juice in each serving bowl. Use a slotted spoon to divide the fish into the bowls. Slice up the remaining quarter cucumber and arrange it on the fish; top with orange segments, jicama, red onion, avocado, basil, and a pinch of flaky sea salt each. Serve with corn or taro chips.

POKE BOWL

SERVES: 4 // TOTAL TIME: 5 minutes

1 lb sushi-grade, wild-caught bluefin tuna, or fish of choice

1 Tablespoon non-toasted sesame oil

¼ cup gluten-free ponzu

¼ cup chopped chives

1 Tablespoon sesame seeds

Rinse the fish and pat dry with a paper towel. Cut into ½-inch cubes, and place in a bowl. Add the sesame oil and ponzu, toss to coat. Top with chives and sesame seeds.

LOADED POTATO ROUNDS WITH EDAMAME HUMMUS

SERVES: 5-8 // TOTAL TIME: 25 minutes

This is a great dish to make for a party. It's beautiful, colorful, and damn good. You can put a little bit of everything on the platter, so you're able to cover any and all dietary restrictions. You can do dairy-free, gluten-free, vegan, and meat lovers' all on one big platter. The topping choices are endless; I like to use sun-dried tomatoes, ground beef, jalapeños, microgreens, onions, cherry tomatoes, and milk-free sour cream.

Potatoes

2 large russet potatoes

2 Tablespoons avocado oil, plus more for baking sheet

Himalayan salt and freshly ground black pepper, to taste

Toppings

Sun-dried tomatoes (optional)

Jalapeño peppers (optional)

Chopped red onions (optional)

Sesame seeds (optional)

Grass-fed ground beef (optional)

Hummus

1 (10-oz) bag frozen shelled edamame, thawed

¼ cup tahini

½ cup chicken stock

2 Tablespoons freshly squeezed lemon juice

4 cloves garlic

1 Tablespoon nutritional yeast

2 Tablespoons non-toasted sesame oil

½ teaspoon Himalayan salt

1. Preheat the oven to 375°F and line a baking sheet with reusable parchment paper.

2. Wash the potatoes and slice them into ¼-inch-thick rounds.

3. Place the rounds onto the baking sheet, drizzle with avocado oil, and sprinkle with salt and pepper. Bake for 14 minutes.

4. Meanwhile, make the hummus: Place all of the ingredients in a food processor or blender, and blend on high until smooth, about 1 minute.

5. Turn the heat up to 500°F. Put the potatoes on the top rack and bake the potato rounds for 1–2 minutes more for a little extra crisp. Monitor them closely to make sure they don't burn.

6. Remove potato rounds and let cool for a few minutes before topping with edamame hummus and whatever toppings you choose.

BACON-WRAPPED DATES STUFFED WITH GOAT CHEESE

MAKES: 16 // TOTAL TIME: 35 minutes

I don't normally eat goat cheese but these are worth it. They're just the right amount of sweet and savory. These can be served as an appetizer or as a dessert, and they're sure to be a crowd pleaser. I like to use thick-cut bacon from the deli, as it gets crispy and adds big flavor. If you use thin bacon, the overall time will be cut down by a few minutes, since it won't take as long to cook.

8 slices applewood-smoked thick-cut bacon

16 Medjool dates

4 ounces fresh goat cheese

1. Preheat the oven to 375°F and line a rimmed baking sheet with reusable parchment paper.

2. Slice the dates in half lengthwise and take out the pits. Cut the bacon slices in half crosswise.

3. Stuff each date with about a teaspoon of goat cheese, place the top halves back on, and wrap with bacon. Secure the bacon with a toothpick and place dates on the baking sheet.

4. Bake for 30 minutes, flipping half way through, or until the bacon is crispy. Time will vary depending on how thick the bacon is.

5. Let drain on a paper towel for a few minutes before serving.

FRIED PICKLES/JALAPEÑOS

SERVES: 4 // TOTAL TIME: 30 minutes

Anyone who knows me well knows that I make these ALL the time. In Texas, fried pickles or jalapeños are a staple on pretty much every menu; here in Cali, not so much. I played around with several recipes and finally landed on one that I love—and so does everyone who has tried them. You would never guess these are gluten-free, and the vegan ranch paired with it tastes even better than regular ranch. These can be baked in the oven or air-fried. If you want a fun twist sub gluten-free pretzels for panko.

Tip: Use Claussen pickle sandwich slices, and you have to use Tofutti milk-free sour cream for the ranch. There are no alternatives that make it taste this good.

12 Claussen pickle sandwich slices or 3 large jalapeños, sliced lengthwise

Avocado oil cooking spray

2 cups gluten-free panko bread crumbs

1 teaspoon onion powder

1 teaspoon garlic salt

2 eggs

1 cup Tofutti milk-free sour cream

2 Tablespoons ranch seasoning (Hidden Valley)

1–2 Tablespoons filtered water

1. Spread the pickles on a paper towel to soak up any extra moisture. Pat the tops dry.

2. Preheat the oven to 400°F and line a baking sheet with reusable parchment paper. If using an air fryer, preheat to 400°F and grease the air fryer rack with cooking spray.

3. Blend the panko, onion powder, and garlic salt in a food processor or blender until powdered. Pour into a wide, shallow bowl. In another wide, shallow bowl, whisk together the eggs.

4. One by one, submerge each pickle or jalapeño into the egg mixture and then into the panko mixture, making sure each pickle or jalapeño is coated; use your fingers to lightly pack the panko mixture on. Arrange the pickles or jalapeños on the baking sheet, making sure to leave enough space between each pickle or jalapeño so they are not touching.

5. Lightly spray the pickles or jalapeños with cooking spray and bake for 15 minutes, or until golden brown.

6. If using the air fryer, arrange pickles or jalapeños in a single layer (no overlapping). Give them all a quick spray of cooking spray and air fry until golden brown, about 16-18 minutes.

7. While those are in the oven, make the ranch: In a small bowl, whisk the sour cream, ranch seasoning, and 1 Tablespoon of water together. If you want a thinner consistency, add more water 1 Tablespoon at a time, whisking until you have your desired consistency.

8. Serve immediately with ranch.

BLISTERED SHISHITOS

SERVES: 4 // TOTAL TIME: 5 minutes

I always order shishitos at sushi restaurants and eat them while we wait on our food. Since we have a big garden, I started growing them at home. In the summer and fall the plant produces tons of peppers. I love to be able to head out to the garden and pick a handful, bring them inside, and sauté them up. These make for a great, quick-and-easy appetizer. They're best eaten right off the skillet.

2 Tablespoons truffle oil

3 cups shishito peppers, washed and dried

Flaky sea salt

1. Heat the truffle oil in a large skillet over medium heat.

2. Place the shishitos in the skillet and cook until they start to blister, stirring occasionally so they blister evenly, about 3–4 minutes.

3. Sprinkle with flaky sea salt and serve immediately.

MEAT

SHREDDED CHICKEN-ZUCCHINI ENCHILADAS

SERVES: 4 // TOTAL TIME: 1 hour

I have a special place in my heart for Tex-Mex. I grew up and spent most of my life in Texas. When I had to go dairy-free, I thought I would have to kiss Tex-Mex goodbye. I mean, how can you eat enchiladas, nachos, or queso without cheese? But I soon found out they're all possible. I love to use the Crock-Pot and slow-cook chicken so it's easy to shred, but if you're in a hurry, you can always quick-cook your chicken and shred with a hand mixer or food processor.

2 boneless, skinless, air-chilled chicken breasts

2–3 cups chicken stock

½ teaspoon sea salt, plus more to taste

Freshly ground black pepper, to taste

3 large zucchinis

2 Tablespoons avocado oil, plus more for dish

1 white onion, chopped fine

2 teaspoons ground cumin

2 teaspoons chili powder

4 cloves garlic, minced

1 ½ cups green or red enchilada sauce

1 cup shredded dairy-free Monterey jack cheese

1 cup shredded dairy-free cheddar cheese

Tofutti milk-free sour cream, for serving

Hot sauce, for serving

Sliced avocado, for serving

Sliced jalapeño peppers, for serving

1. There are two ways to cook your chicken:
• Slow-cook: See page 105
• Bake. Preheat the oven to 400°F. Place the chicken breasts in a glass baking dish and cover them half way up with chicken stock. Lightly salt and pepper the chicken. Bake uncovered for 20–25 minutes, or until cooked through.

2. If your chicken is very tender, you can shred it with two forks. If you baked your chicken and it isn't shredding easily, cut the breasts in half and use a hand mixer or a food processor to shred.

3. Preheat the oven to 375°F and grease an 8x10-inch baking dish.

4. Slice the zucchini lengthwise with a mandoline or a Y peeler into thin slices (ideally about ⅛ inch; they should be thick enough to hold the weight of the enchilada but thin enough to roll up). Lay the zucchini strips flat, and lightly salt them to release some moisture. Let them sit for 10 minutes before dabbing dry with paper towels. Soggy zucchini is not your friend.

5. Heat up the avocado oil in a large skillet over medium heat. Sauté the chopped onion in the oil for around 5 minutes, stirring occasionally. Add in the cumin, chili powder, garlic, and ½ teaspoon salt. Sauté, stirring often, until fragrant, about 1 minute. Add in the shredded chicken and 1 cup of the enchilada sauce and stir until well combined; cook about 1–2 minutes to heat through.

6. Lay out 3 slices of zucchini so they're slightly overlapping, and place a spoonful of chicken mixture at one end. Roll up the zucchini like a tortilla and place in the greased baking dish. Repeat with the remaining zucchini.

7. If there is any chicken mixture left over, pour it over the top. Pour the rest of the enchilada sauce over the top and sprinkle with dairy-free cheese.

8. Cover with foil and bake for 30 minutes. Dairy-free cheese takes a little longer to melt. Serve with a side of milk-free sour cream, your favorite hot sauce, sliced avocado, and sliced jalapeños.

EASY SLOW-COOKER CHICKEN

SERVES: 4-6 // TOTAL TIME: 4 hours

Shredded is by far my favorite way to eat chicken and this recipe will have it shredding on its own without you having to do all the work. It's so easy to pop in the Crock-Pot in the morning and let it cook all day while you're working. When you get home, you will have perfectly moist, falling-apart chicken to add to whatever you please. I love having shredded chicken on hand in the fridge; it makes whipping up some of the recipes I like to make super easy and quick.

2–4 boneless, skinless, air-chilled chicken breasts

2–4 cups chicken stock

Himalayan salt and freshly ground black pepper, to taste

Tip: When reheating the chicken, use the stove top; do not microwave. Add all of the chicken stock into the skillet along with the chicken, and heat it over medium heat.

1. Place the chicken breasts in the Crock-Pot. Pour in enough chicken stock to almost cover the breasts, and salt and pepper the breasts to your liking.

2. Slow-cook on low for at least 4 hours. You can start them in the morning and let them slow-cook all day. The longer you cook them the more tender the chicken will be.

3. Once they are ready, you can either shred with two forks or chop the breasts in half and use a hand mixer or pulse in a food processor until shredded.

4. Store leftover chicken and stock in the fridge in an airtight container for up to 5 days.

CASHEW CHICKEN

SERVES: 4 // TOTAL TIME: 25 minutes

Cashew chicken, who doesn't like it? This was my go-to whenever I ate at a Chinese restaurant, but I would always come home feeling bogged down and stuffy because of all the gluten and MSG. This is a lighter version that is full of flavor and cuts out all of the BS. If you want to reduce dishes, you can use one skillet for the entire process. Once the chicken is cooked, set it aside in a bowl while the veggies are cooking, and then toss it back in. You can reuse that bowl for serving.

2 cups white or brown rice

Avocado oil cooking spray

Himalayan salt and freshly ground black pepper, to taste

2 boneless, skinless, air-chilled chicken breasts, sliced in half lengthwise and into thin strips

3 Tablespoons non-toasted sesame oil

1 crown of broccoli, cut into florets

1 cup snow peas

1 zucchini, sliced into 3-inch spears

3 cloves garlic, minced

2 cups green or red cabbage, chopped

½ white onion, sliced

½ cup raw cashews, for garnish

Sesame seeds, for garnish

Stir Fry Sauce

¼ cup tamari

¼ cup chicken stock

1 Tablespoon local, raw honey

2 cloves garlic, minced

1-inch piece ginger, peeled and grated

1 Tablespoon non-toasted sesame oil

1 teaspoon rice vinegar

1 Tablespoon crushed red pepper

1. Cook the rice according to package instructions.

2. Meanwhile, make the stir-fry sauce: In a small bowl, whisk together all of the sauce ingredients until well combined.

3. Spray a large skillet with cooking spray and place over medium heat. Salt and pepper the chicken and add to the hot skillet. Cook for 6–8 minutes, stirring occasionally, until the chicken is cooked through.

4. In a wok or separate skillet, heat 2 Tablespoons of the sesame oil over medium heat. Add in the broccoli and snow peas and let cook for 3–5 minutes, stirring occasionally.

5. Add the remaining 1 Tablespoon sesame oil to the wok or skillet and add the zucchini, garlic, cabbage, onions, chicken, and ¼ cup of the stir-fry sauce. Cook for another 3–5 minutes, stirring occasionally.

6. Garnish with cashews and sesame seeds, and serve with rice. Place the rest of the stir-fry sauce on the table for serving.

PRETZEL CHICKEN TENDERS

SERVES: 4 // TOTAL TIME: 30 minutes

Holy chicken tenders, these are amazing! But who says they have to be bad for you? Fried chicken gets made at our house several times a week. I always use Glutino gluten-free pretzels, but you can use any brand you like. I sometimes use honey-mustard pretzels to give it a little extra flavor. Check out the recipes for dairy-free ranch, honey mustard, and hot honey sauce for dippin'. If you're not a big pretzel fan, you can change the breading up. You can use gluten-free panko, or I have added an alternative coconut tender recipe.

Avocado oil cooking spray

2 eggs

8 oz bag of gluten-free pretzels (Glutino)

1 teaspoon garlic salt

1 teaspoon onion powder

1 teaspoon paprika

1 teaspoon freshly ground black pepper

2 lbs boneless, skinless, air-chilled chicken breasts, cut into tenders

Hot Honey Sauce (pg. 171)

Ranch Sauce for Dippin' (pg. 170)

Honey Mustard Sauce (pg. 171)

1. Preheat the oven to 425°F and line a baking sheet with reusable parchment paper. If using an air fryer, preheat to 400°F and grease the air fryer rack with cooking spray.

2. In a food processor or blender, blend the pretzels until they are powdered with some slightly larger crumbles for crunchiness. You want about 2 cups crushed pretzels.

3. Place the pretzel crumbs, garlic salt, onion powder, paprika, and pepper in a wide, shallow bowl and mix together. (Alternatively, combine the ingredients for the coconut breading in a bowl.) In another wide, shallow bowl, whisk together the eggs.

4. One by one, submerge each tender into the egg mixture and then into the pretzel mixture, making sure each tender is coated; use your fingers to lightly pack the pretzel mixture on. Arrange the tenders on the baking sheet, making sure to leave enough space between each tender so they are not touching.

5. Lightly spray each tender with cooking spray and bake for 18 minutes. For extra crispiness, turn the oven to broil and cook for another 2 minutes, paying close attention so they do not burn.

6. If using the air fryer, arrange the tenders in a single layer (no overlapping). Give them a quick spray of cooking spray and air fry until golden brown, about 16-18 minutes.

7. Let the chicken cool for a few minutes, then serve with hot honey, ranch, or honey mustard sauces for dippin'.

Coconut Breading Alternative
You can use this breading instead of the pretzel recipe above.

½ cup gluten-free panko bread crumbs
1 ½ cups shredded unsweetened coconut
2 Tablespoons coconut flour
½ teaspoon paprika
1 teaspoon garlic salt
½ teaspoon freshly ground black pepper

1. Place all of the ingredients in a food processor or blender and blend for about 15 seconds, or until the mixture is powdered. Place in a wide, shallow bowl. In another wide, shallow bowl whisk together the eggs.

2. Proceed with step 4.

SPICY CHICKEN TACOS

SERVES: 4 // TOTAL TIME: 45 minutes

Tacos, my favorite food group! Being a native Texan, I grew up on tacos. If I had to choose one food to eat the rest of my life, can you guess what it would be? Tacos! I love to make my own cassava flour tortillas, but don't feel you need to if you don't want to. You can buy gluten-free tortillas and go from there, though I can't promise they will be as good.

Tip: I always grind my own chicken breasts in a food processor; that way I know I'm getting good-quality meat. Cut the raw breast in half and toss into the food processor; blend on high until the chicken is ground.

12 cassava flour tortillas (pg. 194) or any gluten-free tortillas

2 boneless, skinless, air-chilled chicken breasts (my preference) or 1 lb ground chicken

2 Tablespoons avocado oil

½ white onion, chopped

2 Tablespoons chili powder

2 teaspoons smoked paprika

2 teaspoons ground cumin

1 teaspoon garlic salt

1 teaspoon crushed red pepper

1 teaspoon onion powder

¾ cup filtered water

½ cup shredded, dairy-free cheddar cheese

Avocado oil cooking spray

Toppings

Lettuce, shredded (optional)

1 jalapeño pepper, chopped (optional)

1 firm, ripe avocado, peeled, pitted and cubed (optional)

Ranch Sauce for Dippin' (pg. 170)

1. Preheat the oven to 400°F and line a rimmed baking sheet with reusable parchment paper. If using, make the cassava flour tortillas according to instructions on pg. 194. If starting with chicken breasts, cut them in half and place in a food processor. Blend on high until the chicken is ground.

2. In a large skillet, heat the avocado oil over medium-high heat. Add the ground chicken and onion. Cook the chicken, breaking it apart as it cooks, about 5 minutes. Add the chili powder, paprika, cumin, garlic salt, red pepper flakes, and onion powder and stir to combine.

3. Add the water and reduce the heat to medium. Simmer for 10 minutes. The liquid will thicken slightly.

4. Meanwhile, carefully spray the tortillas with cooking spray and drape each tortilla over two wires of the oven rack with the edges hanging down to create a taco-shell shape. Let bake for about 8-10 minutes, then carefully remove.

5. Line the taco shells up on the baking sheet, using the rims to help hold them upright. Divide the meat among the taco shells and top with a sprinkle of dairy-free cheese. Bake for another 10 minutes.

6. Top the tacos with whatever you like. I like lettuce, jalapeño, avocado, and vegan ranch.

COCONUT-LIME CHICKEN CURRY

SERVES: 4 // TOTAL TIME: 25 minutes

Back in 2014, I lived in Thailand for a few months, and I fell in love with the food. This curry dish brings me back to those days spent wandering around the streets and stopping into little local restaurants to try out their food. Coconut milk is a great alternative for anyone cutting out dairy.

1 cup white or brown rice

1 Tablespoon coconut oil

2 boneless, skinless, air-chilled chicken breasts

1 teaspoon onion powder

1 teaspoon garlic salt

1 teaspoon curry powder

1 (13.5-oz) can full-fat coconut milk

½ cup chicken stock

1 Tablespoon local, raw honey

3 Tablespoons green curry paste

Juice of 1 lime

1 Tablespoon sriracha

Basil, for garnish

Grated lime zest, for garnish

1. Cook rice according to the package instructions.

2. In a large skillet, melt the coconut oil over medium heat. Slice the chicken breasts in half horizontally so they'll cook quicker.

3. In a wide, shallow bowl, mix together the onion powder, garlic salt, and curry powder. Lay the chicken into the seasoning and flip it so the entire breast if covered. Repeat for remaining breasts.

4. Once hot, place the seasoned breasts in the skillet, being careful not to overlap. Cook for about 3 minutes on each side, or until lightly browned. Set aside on a plate.

5. In a medium bowl, whisk the coconut milk, chicken stock, honey, green curry paste, lime juice, and sriracha together until well combined.

6. Pour the mixture into the same skillet and bring to a slight boil, scraping up any browned bits from the chicken and mixing them into the sauce.

7. Place the chicken back in the skillet and turn the heat to low. Cover and let simmer for another 5 minutes.

8. Build your bowl starting with rice, then chicken, and sauce poured over the top. Garnish with basil and lime zest.

BAKED LEMON & GARLIC CHICKEN

SERVES: 4 // TOTAL TIME: 40 minutes

Lemon, garlic, and butter are 3 of my favorite things. This is one of the most popular dishes at our house. The kids love it, my husband loves it, and it's great for large groups, because it's easy to make in bulk. It can be served over a bed of rice or just with a sautéed vegetable. I love to use Kerrygold grass-fed butter. It's the one dairy item that does not bother my stomach. In fact, it's tolerated in a lot of dairy-free diets, since it only contains a small trace of lactose. If you have a severe allergy and can't tolerate it, you can always sub for dairy-free butter. Earth Balance is my favorite dairy-free butter.

1 cup white or brown rice

Avocado oil cooking spray

2 boneless, skinless, air-chilled chicken breasts

¼ cup Trader Joe's 21 Seasoning Salute

5 Tablespoons Kerrygold butter or dairy-free butter, softened

5 cloves garlic, minced

½ cup chicken stock

Juice of 2 lemons

Lemon slices, for serving

1. Cook rice according to the package instructions.

2. Preheat the oven to 400°F. Spray a large skillet with cooking spray and heat it over medium-high heat.

3. Slice the chicken breasts in half horizontally so they cook quicker. In a wide, shallow bowl, add the 21 Seasoning Salute. Lay the chicken into the seasoning and flip so the entire breast is covered. Repeat for remaining breasts.

4. Once hot, place the seasoned breasts in the skillet, being careful not to overlap, and cook for 3 minutes on each side, or until lightly browned.

5. Meanwhile, in a small bowl, whisk together the melted butter, minced garlic, chicken stock, and lemon juice.

6. Transfer the chicken to a baking dish, and pour the butter mixture over the chicken. Bake uncovered for 25 minutes.

7. Build your bowl: first the rice, then the chicken. Spoon the sauce from the baking dish over the top of the chicken and garnish each bowl with a lemon slice.

Tip: If you don't have 21 Seasoning Salute, you can use Italian seasoning or lemon pepper in its place.

THAI CHICKEN LETTUCE WRAPS

SERVES: 4 // TOTAL TIME: 30 minutes

These are such a hit anytime I make them. They're low-carb, healthy, and oh-so-good. They're easy to make and can be served as an appetizer or as a meal. You can make them vegetarian by taking out the meat and adding more veggies. I like this combo of veggies, but you can add other veggies such as mushrooms, eggplant, or cabbage.

Tip: Grinding your own chicken at home is quick and easy. It also ensures that you are getting high-quality lean white meat.

2 boneless, skinless, air-chilled chicken breasts (my preference) or 1 lb ground chicken

Avocado oil cooking spray

1 Tablespoon non-toasted sesame oil

1 zucchini, chopped

1 large carrot, peeled and chopped

½ white onion, chopped

2 cups baby spinach leaves

1 (8 oz) can water chestnuts, chopped

8 whole leaves romaine lettuce, washed and dried

Sesame seeds, for garnish

Sauce

½ cup rice vinegar

½ cup tamari, or any gluten-free soy sauce

1-inch piece of ginger, peeled and chopped small

1 teaspoon crushed red pepper

1 Tablespoon local, raw honey

4 cloves garlic, minced

1. If using chicken breasts, cut them in half and place in a food processor. Blend on high until the chicken is ground.

2. Spray a large skillet over medium heat with cooking spray. Add the ground chicken and cook, breaking it apart as it cooks, for 5–6 minutes, or until cooked through. Remove to a bowl.

3. Heat 1 Tablespoon sesame oil in the same skillet. Add the zucchini, carrots, and onions. Cook for 5 minutes, or until slightly tender.

4. Meanwhile, make the sauce: In a small bowl, whisk together all of the sauce ingredients until well combined.

5. Add the cooked chicken, spinach, and water chestnuts into the skillet with the veggies. Pour half of the sauce over the top, reduce heat to low, and cook for another 5 minutes.

6. Serve immediately. Place the lettuce on a separate platter, put out the remaining sauce and sesame seeds for topping, and let everyone build their own lettuce wrap.

CHICKEN VERMICELLI BOWL

SERVES: 4 // TOTAL TIME: 30 minutes

I lived in Vietnam for a little bit back in 2014, and damn, they have good food. When I returned to Austin, I had a hard time finding authentic Vietnamese food. There was one place down the street from my old house that had awesome vermicelli bowls. Now that I've moved to Cali, I miss that little restaurant and their bowls. After much trial and error, I've come up with my own version for all of you to enjoy. You can take out the chicken and add more veggies for a vegan dish or sub shrimp to make it pescatarian.

2 cups chicken stock

Himalayan salt and freshly ground black pepper, to taste

1 boneless, skinless, air-chilled chicken breast, sliced into small chunks

8 oz dried Vietnamese rice vermicelli noodles

1 crown broccoli, cut into florets

¼ cup filtered water

1 cup bean sprouts

2 cups iceberg lettuce, chopped

1 carrot, peeled and shaved

⅛ white onion, sliced

1 firm, ripe avocado, peeled, pitted and sliced

1 jalapeño pepper, sliced (optional)

Sauce

¼ cup freshly squeezed lime juice

1 Tablespoon rice vinegar

3 Tablespoons coconut or turbinado sugar

⅔ cup filtered water

⅓ cup fish sauce

1–3 Thai chilies (very spicy!)

3 cloves garlic, minced

Toppings

Sriracha

Tamari

⅓ cup salted raw peanuts

Handful mint leaves

Handful basil leaves

1. In a medium pot over high heat, bring the chicken stock to a boil.

2. Salt and pepper the chicken chunks and add them to the pot. Reduce the temperature to medium, and let cook uncovered for 8–10 minutes, or until the chicken is cooked through. Remove from heat, strain, and set aside.

3. Meanwhile, place all of the sauce ingredients into a small bowl and whisk until well combined.

4. Cook the noodles according to the package instructions. Strain, rinse with cold water and place in a bowl for serving.

5. In the meantime, gather all of the raw toppings and place into small bowls for serving.

6. Place the broccoli florets in a small pot with the water. Cover and steam over medium heat until cooked to your desired tenderness, about 4 minutes. Remove from heat, strain if needed, and place in a bowl for serving.

7. Build each bowl starting with the noodles, then sprouts, lettuce, carrots, onions, avocado, jalapeño (if using), and broccoli. Top with chicken. Pour the sauce over the top and add sriracha and tamari to taste. Garnish with peanuts, mint, and basil.

GREEN CURRY

SERVES: 4 // TOTAL TIME: 25 minutes

Green curry is my favorite of all the curries. And the one ingredient that makes the dish so delicious is Thai eggplant. I absolutely love it. Instead of a spongy texture like a regular eggplant, it's a little golf ball–size veggie that has a firm texture and little seeds. It's really hard to find in the store, so I started growing my own. If you can't find Thai eggplant, you can use regular eggplant in its place, sub another one of your favorite veggies, or just take it out altogether. The great thing about curry is you can really put anything in it you like and it will be delicious!

1 cup white or brown rice

2 (13.5-oz) cans full-fat coconut milk

2 (6-oz) cans green curry paste

3 Tablespoons curry powder

2 boneless, skinless, air-chilled chicken breasts, cut into small strips

Himalayan salt and freshly ground black pepper, to taste

1 crown broccoli, cut into florets

2 cups halved fresh green beans

¼ white onion, sliced

½ carrot, peeled and shaved

3 Thai eggplants, quartered

1 (8-oz) can sliced water chestnuts, drained

1 cup bean sprouts

Raw cashews and basil, for garnish (optional)

1. Cook the rice according to the package instructions.

2. In a large pot over high heat, whisk together the coconut milk, curry paste, and curry powder. Bring to a slight boil.

3. Season the chicken with salt and pepper and add to the pot. Reduce heat to medium-low, cover, and let the chicken cook, stirring occasionally, for about 5 minutes, or until cooked through.

4. Add the broccoli florets, green beans, onions, carrots, and Thai eggplants. Stir to combine and let simmer for 3–4 minutes.

5. Add the water chestnuts and bean sprouts, and let simmer for another 2–3 minutes.

6. Build your bowl with rice, then curry, and garnish with cashews and basil.

SWEET POTATO BURRITO BOATS

SERVES: 4-6 // TOTAL TIME: 1 hour 25 minutes

Don't get discouraged by the lengthy cook time on these. It's the potatoes that take a long time to bake. If you're in a pinch, you can cook them in the microwave: Just wrap each potato in a wet paper towel, place them in the microwave, and cook for 10–15 minutes; the time will depend on how many potatoes you're cooking at once and how large they are. I love to make these when we have guests over. They're easy to make in bulk, and they're full of flavor and color.

Potatoes

4 large sweet potatoes

1 Tablespoon avocado oil

Himalayan salt, to taste

Dash of cayenne pepper

2 Tablespoons brown sugar

Sliced habanero peppers, for garnish (optional)

Creamy Dressing

1 cup Tofutti milk-free sour cream

1 Tablespoon local, raw honey

1 Tablespoon avocado or grapeseed oil

Turkey-Black Bean Salsa

1 lb ground turkey

½ teaspoon cayenne pepper

½ teaspoon garlic powder

1 (15-oz) can black beans, rinsed and drained

1 (16-oz) can sweet corn, rinsed and drained

1 cup cherry tomatoes, diced

¼ white onion, diced

3 cloves garlic, minced

2 jalapeño peppers, diced

¼ cup chopped cilantro

¼ cup freshly squeezed lime juice

1 teaspoon garlic salt

1 teaspoon freshly ground black pepper, or to taste

1 Tablespoon avocado or grapeseed oil

Tip: To help drizzle the dressing, spoon it into a small resealable bag and cut the corner off. Squeeze through the hole to drizzle it on the potatoes.

1. Preheat the oven to 400°F and line a baking sheet with reusable parchment paper.

2. Wash the sweet potatoes and pierce each one several times with a fork. Rub each potato with avocado oil and a sprinkle of salt. Place on the lined baking sheet.

3. Bake until sweet potatoes are cooked through but not too soft, a little over 1 hour. Time will vary depending on the size of the potato.

4. Meanwhile, start the turkey-black bean salsa: In a large skillet over medium heat, cook the turkey with cayenne and garlic powder, breaking it apart as it cooks, until it's cooked through, about 5–6 minutes.

5. Combine the cooked turkey and the rest of the ingredients for the salsa in a large bowl and stir to combine.

6. Make the dressing: In a small bowl, whisk the creamy dressing ingredients together until well combined. Set aside.

7. When the potatoes are done and slightly cooled, slit them open and carefully scoop out the center flesh (creating a boat) into a bowl, mashing with a dash of cayenne and the brown sugar. Equally distribute the sweet potato mixture back into the sweet potato boats.

8. Top each potato with the turkey-black bean salsa, and drizzle with the creamy dressing. If you want an extra kick, garnish with habanero.

BEEF AND BROCCOLI

SERVES: 4 // TOTAL TIME: 25 minutes

This is one of the first meals I started cooking when I got my own place. It was an easy meal to make for one, and the leftovers heated up well. Now, over 10 years later, it's still a dish that I love to eat. This dish can be made with ground beef, bison, chicken, or turkey; they're all delicious. The rice is optional; the dish tastes great without it as well.

1 cup of white or brown rice

1 lb ground beef, chicken, bison, or turkey

½ white onion, chopped small

2 cloves garlic, sliced

1 large crown broccoli, cut into florets

2 Tablespoons filtered water

⅓ cup brown sugar

⅓ cup tamari

Chopped chives, for garnish

Sesame seeds, for garnish

1. Cook the rice according to the package instructions.

2. In a large skillet over medium heat, cook the ground meat, onions, and garlic, breaking it apart as it cooks, until cooked through, about 5 minutes. If your meat has a high fat content, strain it.

3. Meanwhile, place the broccoli florets in a small pot with the water. Cover and steam over medium heat until cooked to your desired tenderness, about 4 minutes.

4. Strain the broccoli and chop. Add the chopped broccoli, brown sugar, and tamari to the meat and let simmer, uncovered, for 3 minutes.

5. To build your bowl, start with rice, then add the meat and broccoli. Top with chives and sesame seeds.

MAMMAW'S SPAGHETTI

SERVES: 4 // TOTAL TIME: 1 hour 20 minutes

Growing up, my grandma was always in the kitchen. She loved to cook, and everyone loved to eat what she was serving. My favorite dish that she made was her famous spaghetti. When I was young, I was a very picky eater. When she made spaghetti, I would eat only the noodles and cover them in sugar. I don't think I ever tried the actual meat sauce until I was about 10 years old. Man, was I missing out. As I got older, when my grandma or my mom would make spaghetti for dinner, I would come in and get a bowl of the meat sauce before it was done simmering to test it out before dinner. I still make this sauce to this day, and people always ask me for the recipe. Thanks Mammaw!

1 ½ lb grass-fed ground beef

1 white onion, chopped

1 (28-oz) can diced tomatoes

2 (15-oz) cans tomato sauce

1 (6-oz) can tomato paste

4 cloves garlic, minced

2 bay leaves

1 Tablespoon Worcestershire sauce

2 teaspoons celery salt

2 teaspoons garlic salt

¼ cup brown sugar

¼ cup Italian seasoning

Gluten-free noodles of choice (Taste Republic)

Nutritional yeast, for topping (optional)

1. In a large skillet over medium heat, brown the beef and onions, breaking it apart as it cooks. Strain the fat and put the meat into a large stockpot along with all of the other ingredients (except noodles).

2. Bring to a slight boil, then lower the heat to low. Cover and let simmer for at least an hour, stirring occasionally.

3. When the sauce is almost ready, cook the noodles according to the package instructions. Remember that fresh noodles only need to be cooked about 4 minutes.

4. Serve the meat sauce over the noodles and top with nutritional yeast for a cheesy flavor, if desired.

Tip: This dish is also great served over zoodles (pg. 199) or spaghetti squash.

STIR-FRY

SERVES: 4 // TOTAL TIME: 30 minutes

Stir-fry is a staple at our house. When I am craving a good, healthy dish with a lot of veggies, this is what I make. You can literally throw anything from your veggie drawer into this dish and it will taste amazing. Did you know that most store-bought stir-fry sauces contain gluten and are full of crap? Toss out any store-bought stir-fry sauce you have, and mix up this easy, healthy sauce instead. It's light and refreshing and won't make you feel bloated.

Stir-Fry

1 cup white or brown rice

1 lb filet mignon or 2 boneless, skinless, air chilled chicken breasts

Himalayan salt and freshly ground black pepper, to taste

Avocado oil cooking spray

2 Tablespoons non-toasted sesame oil

1 large crown broccoli, cut into florets

½ white onion, sliced thin

1 (8-oz) can sliced water chestnuts, drained

8 ears baby corn

½ (8-oz) can bamboo shoots, drained

2 cups bean sprouts

1 cup sugar snap peas

3 cloves garlic, sliced thin

Sesame seeds, for garnish

Stir Fry Sauce

½ cup tamari or any gluten-free soy sauce

½ cup chicken stock

1 Tablespoon arrowroot powder

1 Tablespoon local, raw honey

4 cloves garlic, minced

2-inch piece of ginger, peeled and grated

1 Tablespoon non-toasted sesame oil

1 teaspoon rice vinegar

1 Tablespoon crushed red pepper

1. Make the sauce: In a small bowl, whisk together all of the sauce ingredients until well combined.

2. Cook the rice according to the package instructions.

3. If you're making steak: Heat a grill up to 450°F. Season the steak with salt and pepper. For medium-rare, cook the steak on direct heat for 3 minutes on each side, then cook on indirect heat for 3 minutes each side. If you would like it more well-done, keep it on an extra few minutes. Once the steak is done, let it sit for 5 minutes before slicing it thin, against the grain.
For chicken: Spray a large skillet with cooking spray and turn the heat to medium-high. Slice the chicken breasts in half horizontally. Season them lightly with salt and pepper and, once hot, cook on each side for about 3 minutes or until slightly browned. Remove from heat and slice into thin strips; set aside.

4. In a large wok or skillet, heat the sesame oil over medium heat. Add in the broccoli and let cook for 3 minutes, stirring occasionally. Add in the onions, water chestnuts, baby corn, bamboo shoots, bean sprouts, snap peas, garlic, chicken (if using), and half of the stir-fry sauce. Lightly toss and let cook over medium heat for 3–5 minutes, or until the veggies are your desired tenderness. (I tend to sauté my veggies for less time because I like them crunchy.)

5. To make the stir-fry bowls, start with rice on the bottom, add the veggies and steak (if using), and top with sesame seeds. Use the remaining sauce to put on the table for serving. Serve immediately

SLOW-COOKED CARNITAS

SERVES: 10-12 // TOTAL TIME: 10 hours

This recipe basically makes itself, though it tastes like it was a lot of work. It's just a few ingredients all thrown into a Crock-Pot and cooked overnight. I love making this when I know I am going to be working a lot and won't have time to cook extravagant meals. You can add carnitas to nachos, tacos, salads, enchiladas—just about anything you can think of. The kids love it; in our house it goes quick. It's also great for parties.

Juice of 2 large oranges

1 (12-oz) can Dr. Pepper or Coca-Cola

1 Tablespoon garlic salt

1 Tablespoon freshly ground black pepper

1 Tablespoon ground cumin

5 lb pork butt or shoulder

Tip: When reheating the pork, use the stove top; do not microwave. Add the pork and the juices into the skillet, and heat it up over medium heat.

1. Pour the orange juice into the Crock-Pot along with the can of Dr. Pepper or Coca-Cola.

2. In a small bowl, mix together the garlic salt, pepper, and cumin. Use this as a rub to cover all sides of the pork. Place meat in the Crock-Pot, fat side up.

3. Slow-cook the pork for 10–14 hours. The pork will be falling apart. Take the fat layer off with a fork and throw it out.

4. Place the pork in a bowl and shred with 2 forks. Discard any fat that you come across. Do not discard any of the juices. Once the pork is shredded place it back in the juices for serving.

5. You can serve right away or store in the fridge with the juices, in an airtight container for up to 5 days.

POTSTICKER BOWL

SERVES: 4 // TOTAL TIME: 25 minutes

I fell in love with gyoza (pot stickers) in Japan on my honeymoon. Everywhere I went, I had to get gyoza. I was eating it for breakfast, lunch, and dinner. When I returned home, I was determined to make a gluten-free version that was up to par with Japanese gyoza. I looked and looked to find gluten-free gyoza wrappers but couldn't find any. I tried to make my own out of cassava flour, but they were too thick and didn't steam correctly. That resulted in me making it into a bowl, and I love it—it's low carb and just as delicious.

Tip: Your food processor has a shred disk attachment that sits at the top of the processor bowl. Use this to shred the cabbage and carrot. It's a huge time-saver.

1 cup white or brown rice

1 lb ground pork

1 cup finely chopped napa cabbage

½-inch piece fresh ginger, peeled and finely chopped

1 carrot, peeled and finely chopped

¼ white onion, chopped

4 cloves garlic, minced

1 Tablespoon tamari

1 Tablespoon non-toasted sesame oil

1 egg

Avocado oil cooking spray

Sauce

¼ cup tamari

1 Tablespoon non-toasted sesame oil

2 Tablespoons rice vinegar

2 cloves garlic, minced

1 Tablespoon crushed red pepper

1. Cook rice according to package instructions.

2. In a large skillet, cook the pork over medium heat until cooked all the way through, breaking it apart as it cooks. Remove from heat, and strain.

3. While the meat is cooking, in a large bowl, mix together cabbage, ginger, carrots, onions, and garlic. Add the pork when it is done cooking.

4. In a small bowl, whisk together the tamari, sesame oil, and egg. Add this into the pork mixture and stir to combine.

5. Add the pork mixture to the same large skillet and let simmer for 5 minutes, stirring occasionally.

6. Meanwhile, combine all of the ingredients for the sauce into a small bowl, and whisk until well combined.

7. To build your bowl, start with rice, then add the pork mixture, and pour a little sauce over the top.

SEAFOOD

SHRIMP LINGUINI

SERVES: 4 // TOTAL TIME: 25 minutes

This is one of my go-to dishes if I'm wanting something that is super quick. It's so colorful and has a beautiful presentation. You can make this with spaghetti squash, zoodles, or any gluten-free noodle. I love to use the Costco marinated artichoke hearts, as they have such great flavor. If you can't get those, any marinated artichoke hearts in a glass jar will work.

1 lb large wild-caught shrimp, peeled and deveined

1 teaspoon garlic salt

1 teaspoon freshly ground black pepper

1 teaspoon cracked red pepper

½ teaspoon cayenne pepper, optional

Avocado oil cooking spray

9 oz gluten-free linguini (Taste Republic)

½ cup dry-packed sun-dried tomatoes, chopped

½ cup marinated artichoke hearts, chopped

¼ white onion, chopped

3 cups fresh spinach or Swiss chard

½ cup cherry tomatoes, sliced

2 Tablespoons capers

Dressing

½ cup avocado or grapeseed oil

¼ cup white wine vinegar

1 Tablespoon Dijon mustard

1 Tablespoon local, raw honey

1 Tablespoon crushed red pepper

2 cloves garlic, minced

Juice of ½ lemon

1. Rinse the shrimp and pat dry with a paper towel. In a medium bowl, mix together the garlic salt, black pepper, red pepper, and cayenne (if using). Toss the shrimp in the seasoning.

2. Spray a large skillet over medium heat with cooking spray. Once hot, toss in the shrimp and let cook until pink, about 3–5 minutes, flipping occasionally. Remove to a plate with tongs.

3. Cook linguini according to package instructions. If the noodles are fresh, note that they will only need to be cooked for about 4 minutes.

4. Place the sun-dried tomatoes, artichoke hearts, onions, spinach, and cherry tomatoes in a large serving bowl.

5. Strain the pasta and pour over the top of the veggies. This will slightly steam the veggies.

6. Make the dressing by combining all of the ingredients into a small bowl, and whisk until well combined.

7. Cut the shrimp in half crosswise and add to the serving bowl. Pour half of the dressing over the top and gently toss to combine. Top with capers.

8. Place the other half of the dressing on the table, and serve immediately.

LEMONGRASS-COCONUT SCALLOPS

SERVES: 4 // TOTAL TIME: 25 minutes

My husband loves scallops. Funny to think that I had never tried them before I met him, and I had definitely never cooked any before. One day I wanted to surprise him, so I invited my girlfriend over and we started playing around with some recipes. This is how the lemongrass-coconut scallop dish was created. Lemongrass is one of those flavors that, when I see it on the menu, I order it. I love it so much, I started growing it in our backyard. There are so many dishes and drinks that it goes well in. I love to be able to go down to the garden and snip off a stalk for a fun dish or drink.

---

1 cup white or brown rice

1 shallot, finely sliced

¼ cup white vinegar

1 (13.5-oz) can full-fat coconut milk

Grated zest of 1 lime

2 stalks fresh lemongrass, cut into 3-inch pieces and smashed

1-inch piece of ginger, peeled and sliced

1 teaspoon fish sauce

Juice of 1 lime

2 serrano peppers, sliced

1 Tablespoon coconut oil

8 large, wild-caught sea scallops

Himalayan salt and freshly ground black pepper, to taste

Basil leaves julienned, for garnish

1. Cook rice according to package instructions.

2. In a small pot on low heat, simmer the shallot in vinegar until almost all of the liquid is gone, about 5 minutes.

3. Add coconut milk, half of the lime zest, the smashed lemongrass, and ginger and simmer on low heat for about 5 minutes. Be careful to not let it boil over.

4. Stir in the fish sauce and lime juice. Turn the heat off and add the serrano slices. Let it sit and infuse while you finish cooking.

5. Heat a skillet over medium-high heat. Rinse the scallops and pat dry with a paper towel. Season with a pinch of salt and pepper. Once the skillet is hot, add in the coconut oil. Sear the scallops for about 2 minutes on each side, or until they have a nice golden color. Remove from heat.

6. Quickly heat the lemongrass sauce back up and strain into a small bowl.

7. Assemble the bowls starting with rice, then scallops, and top with lemongrass sauce. Garnish with the remaining lime zest and basil.

Tips: To smash lemongrass, cut off the tough bottom part and the top skinny part. Peel off the tough layers (you can cut a small slit down the stalk to help you peel it off). Once you're left with the inner part, lay it on a cutting board and smash it with a rolling pin or something similar; this will bring all of the juices out.

To julienne basil, stack the leaves, roll them up like a cigar, and slice. This helps keep the oils intact and saves the flavor.

HONEY-BAKED SALMON

SERVES: 2 // TOTAL TIME: 20 minutes

This is another one of those recipes that has stuck with me for years. It's super simple and was easy to make for a party of one. I have no idea why I started cooking salmon this way, but I've continued to do it throughout the years because it's delicious. The sweet-salty-tangy combo gives it such a kick of flavor. This meal pairs great with sautéed asparagus.

1 lb wild-caught salmon filet

2 Tablespoons white wine vinegar

1 Tablespoon local, raw honey

½ teaspoon garlic salt

½ teaspoon freshly ground black pepper

Juice of ½ lemon

Lemon slices, for garnish

1. Preheat the oven to 425°F and rip off a large piece of foil.

2. Rinse the salmon and pat dry with a paper towel. Place it right in the center of the foil. Pour the vinegar over the top of the salmon and add a drizzle of honey, the garlic salt, and pepper.

3. Close the foil over the salmon either by using a second piece or folding over the edges of the large piece. Make sure to crimp the edges, sealing it so the juices don't leak out.

4. Put the foil wrapped salmon in the oven directly on the rack. Bake for 12–14 minutes, or until the salmon flakes apart when poked with a fork.

5. Squeeze the lemon over the top, and serve immediately garnished with lemon slices.

LEMON ZOODLES WITH SALMON

SERVES: 2 // TOTAL TIME: 20 minutes

Spiralizing vegetables is such a fun way to replace noodles. I love spiralizing zucchini and butternut squash, and both of them are delicious in this recipe. I use a thicker setting on the spiralizer so the noodles don't get mushy. This salmon dish is so light and refreshing, with a kick of flavor.

Fish

1 Tablespoon avocado or grapeseed oil

10 ounces wild-caught salmon or fish of choice

Pinch of sea salt and freshly ground black pepper

½ cup cherry tomatoes, sliced

Crushed red pepper, for garnish

2 cloves garlic, sliced thin, for garnish

Zoodles

1 Tablespoon avocado or grapeseed oil

1 shallot, sliced thin

4 cloves garlic, minced

3 large zucchinis, spiralized

Pinch of sea salt and freshly ground black pepper

Grated zest of 1 lemon

1 Tablespoon freshly squeezed lemon juice

1. Preheat the oven to 375°F and line a baking sheet with reusable parchment paper.

2. In a medium skillet over medium-high heat, heat 1 Tablespoon avocado or grapeseed oil until hot.

3. Rinse the fish and pat dry with a paper towel. Sear the fish in the skillet on both sides until golden brown, about 3 minutes per side.

4. Place the fish on the baking sheet and put in the oven to bake for 5–6 minutes, depending on the thickness of the fish, until the salmon flakes apart when poked with a fork.

5. Meanwhile, prepare the zoodles: Heat 1 Tablespoon avocado or grapeseed oil over medium heat, and add the shallot and garlic, stirring frequently to ensure it doesn't burn. Add the spiralized zoodles and season with salt and pepper. Sauté the zoodles until they start to soften, about 4 minutes. Add the lemon zest, lemon juice, and basil, and give it one more quick toss. Remove from heat.

6. Serve the zoodles with the salmon on top, topped with sliced cherry tomatoes, and garnished with crushed red pepper and sliced garlic.

SALT-CRUSTED WHOLE BRANZINO

SERVES: 4 // TOTAL TIME: 1 hour 35 minutes

I fell in love with this spectacular dish in Mexico. I was on vacation in Isla Mujeres and saw it on the menu. I had never heard of it before so I decided to give it a try. They brought it out on a huge platter, cracked it open, and filleted it right in front of us. It blew my mind how tasty the fish was. Fast forward eight years; I had it again in Tulum and I had the same amazing experience. This was something that I had to recreate. This lemony, garlicky fish is so tasty. Cracking open the salt crust to reveal the cooked fish really provides a wow factor if you're having people over.

2 lb rock salt

5 egg whites, whisked

1.5 lb–2 lb whole, wild-caught branzino

6 thin lemon slices

4 cloves garlic, sliced

Chopped garlic, for garnish

Butter Sauce

4 Tablespoons Kerrygold or dairy-free butter, melted

1 teaspoon garlic salt

¼ cup freshly squeezed lemon juice

1. Preheat the oven to 400°F and line a baking sheet, big enough to fit the entire fish, with reusable parchment paper.

2. In a large bowl, combine the salt and egg whites, mixing until it forms a grainy paste. Press a ¼-inch layer of the paste on the reusable parchment paper big enough for the whole fish to lie on.

3. Rinse the fish and pat dry with a paper towel. Stuff the cavity with 4 lemon slices and all of the garlic cloves. Place the fish on the salt paste slab on the baking sheet. Pack remaining salt mixture over the fish to enclose it completely.

4. Bake for 20 minutes, or until the crust is a light golden brown. Remove the fish from the oven, and let sit for 5 minutes before breaking open the salt crust.

5. Meanwhile, make the butter sauce: In a small bowl, combine the butter, garlic salt, and lemon juice, and whisk until well combined.

6. Crack open the salt crust by knocking on it with a spoon. Remove the salt from the top of the fish and discard the head, tail and skin. Slide a fork under the top filet, over the spine, and place the filet on a serving platter. Turn the fish over and repeat; discard any bones.

7. Garnish the fish with lemon slices and chopped garlic. Serve with the butter sauce for dipping.

COCONUT SHRIMP

MAKES: 15-20 // TOTAL TIME: 30 minutes

Coconut shrimp was another dish that I was super bummed to never be able to eat again. It was one of my favorite things to order when I went to a seafood restaurant. I've created a delicious, crispy, gluten-free version that is a healthy alternative to your regular, gluten-packed coconut shrimp. You've got to try them with the hot honey sauce. It's by far my favorite dipping sauce! These are also amazing in tacos!

Avocado oil cooking spray

1 lb large wild-caught shrimp, peeled and deveined

1 cup shredded, unsweetened coconut

1 cup gluten-free panko bread crumbs

½ teaspoon paprika

1 teaspoon garlic salt

½ teaspoon freshly ground black pepper

2 eggs

Hot Honey Sauce

2 Tablespoons Kerrygold or dairy-free butter

½ cup local, raw honey

1-2 Tablespoon cayenne pepper, depending on your spice tolerance

1. Preheat the oven to 425°F and line a baking sheet with reusable parchment paper. If using an air fryer, preheat to 400°F and grease the air fryer rack with cooking spray. Rinse the shrimp and pat dry with a paper towel.

2. In a blender or food processor, blend the panko and coconut on high until powdered.

3. In a wide, shallow bowl, combine the powdered coconut mixture, paprika, garlic salt, and pepper. Mix together until well combined. In another wide, shallow bowl, whisk together the eggs.

4. One by one, submerge each shrimp into the egg mixture and then into the coconut mixture, making sure the entire shrimp is coated; use your fingers to lightly pack the coconut mixture on. Arrange the shrimp on the baking sheet, making sure to leave enough space between each shrimp so they are not touching.

5. Lightly spray the shrimp with cooking spray, and bake for 15–18 minutes.

6. If using the air fryer, arrange shrimp in a single layer (no overlapping). Give them a quick spray of cooking spray and air fry until golden brown, about 16-18 minutes.

7. To make the hot honey sauce, soften the butter in the microwave in a glass bowl for about 20 seconds. Whisk in the honey and cayenne. Serve the shrimp with hot honey sauce.

Tip: You can use all shredded coconut if you don't have gluten-free bread crumbs and they are just as delicious .

FISH TACOS

SERVES: 4 // TOTAL TIME: 40 minutes

Between Texas, California, and my many visits to Mexico, I've spent most of my life in places where fish tacos are standard fare. I can't imagine life without them, but between the breading of the fish, the crema dressing, and the flour tortillas, they became a no-go for me. This is a totally guilt-free, dairy-free, gluten-free fish taco that is sure to make your taste buds happy.

1 lb wild-caught grouper or white fish of choice

½ teaspoon ground cumin

½ teaspoon cayenne pepper

½ teaspoon garlic salt

½ teaspoon freshly ground black pepper

1 Tablespoon avocado or grapeseed oil

1 Tablespoon Kerrygold or dairy-free butter, cut into small cubes

8–10 cassava flour tortillas (pg. 194) or gluten-free tortilla of choice

Toppings

½ cup red cabbage, thinly sliced

¼ red onion, sliced thin

½ cup cherry tomatoes, sliced

½ cup cilantro, chopped

1 firm, ripe avocado, peeled, pitted and sliced thin

Lime wedges

Taco Sauce

½ cup Tofutti milk-free sour cream

⅓ cup mayonnaise

2 Tablespoons freshly squeezed lime juice

½ teaspoon garlic salt

1 teaspoon sriracha

1. Preheat the oven to 375°F and line a rimmed baking sheet with reusable parchment paper. Rinse the fish and pat dry with a paper towel.

2. In wide, shallow bowl, mix together the cumin, cayenne, garlic salt, and pepper. Lay the fish into the seasoning then flip so that the entire fish is covered. Place the fish on the rimmed baking sheet.

3. Lightly drizzle the fish with avocado or grapeseed oil, and arrange the cubes of butter on top. Bake for 20–25 minutes, or until the fish flakes apart when poked with a fork. Time will vary depending on the thickness of the fish.

4. Meanwhile, prep all of the toppings and place in small bowls for serving on the table. If using, make the cassava flour tortillas according to instructions on pg. 194.

5. In a small bowl, whisk the ingredients for the sauce together until well combined. If you want an extra kick, add more sriracha. Set aside.

6. If you're using store bought tortillas, quickly heat them up on a hot, dry, large skillet, about 30 seconds on each side, and store in a tortilla warmer.

7. Place fish, tortillas, toppings, and sauce on the table, and let everyone build their own tacos.

LOBSTER TAILS

MAKES: 2 tails // TOTAL TIME: 30 minutes

Impressive yet simple, these are perfect for a special date night at home, or a more relaxed dinner on the patio.

2 raw, wild-caught lobster tails

2 Tablespoons Kerrygold or dairy-free butter, at room temperature, plus more for dipping

½ teaspoon garlic salt

½ teaspoon freshly ground black pepper

1. Preheat the oven to 425°F and line a rimmed baking sheet with reusable parchment paper.

2. Using a pair of sharp kitchen scissors, cut the top of the shell down the middle almost to the tail fin. Use your fingers to pull the meat out of the tail, being careful not to detach the meat from the tail fin, and place it on top of the cut part of the shell. It should look like the photo.

3. Put 1 Tablespoon of butter on each tail and season with garlic salt and pepper. Place the tails on the baking sheet and bake for 8–10 minutes. A good rule of thumb is to bake the tails 1–2 minutes per ounce. You want the meat to be firm but not overcooked.

4. Serve with melted butter for dipping.

SIDES

SAUTÉED KALE & PEARS

SERVES: 4 // TOTAL TIME: 15 minutes

One of the leafy greens that grows like crazy in our garden is kale. We always have a surplus of it, so it tends to be on the menu a lot at our house. This flavorful combo will even have your kids wanting a bite. The pears give it such great flavor, and when they're cooked in the balsamic, they taste almost like a dessert. If you're able to have goat cheese, it puts this dish over the top!

1 big bunch of kale

2 Tablespoons avocado or grapeseed oil

1 ripe Bosc pear, chopped into cubes

3 Tablespoons balsamic vinegar

Handful crushed walnuts

¼ cup goat cheese crumbles (optional)

1. Wash the kale and cut out the ribs. Discard into your compost bin or trash can. Chop the leaves into 4-inch pieces, and dab any excess water with a paper towel.

2. In a large skillet, heat the oil over medium heat. Add the pear, then the kale, balsamic, and walnuts. Use tongs to mix the balsamic throughout.

3. Sauté for 5 minutes, or until the kale is slightly wilted and the pears are soft.

4. Top with goat cheese crumbles (if using) and serve immediately.

CAULIFLOWER-GARLIC MASHED POTATOES

SERVES: 4 // TOTAL TIME: 15 minutes

I love mashed potatoes and still eat them, but it's nice to have a low-carb option as well. I've fed these to the kids, and they had no idea they were eating cauliflower. The nutritional yeast gives it a cheesy flavor, and the butter makes it super creamy. Pair this with any main dish, and you will not be disappointed.

1 head cauliflower, cored and cut into florets

¼ cup filtered water

1 Tablespoon avocado or grapeseed oil

3 cloves garlic

2 Tablespoons Kerrygold or dairy-free butter

2 Tablespoons nutritional yeast

2 Tablespoons dairy-free cream cheese (Kite Hill)

½ teaspoon sea salt, plus more to taste

½ teaspoon freshly ground black pepper, plus more to taste

1. Place the cauliflower florets in a pot with the water. Turn to medium-high heat, cover, and let steam for 8 minutes, or until tender.

2. Meanwhile, heat the avocado or grapeseed oil in a small skillet over medium heat. Sauté the garlic, stirring often, until fragrant, about 2 minutes. Remove from heat and set aside.

3. Transfer half of the cauliflower florets into a food processor, and blend on high until smooth. Add remaining florets, and blend until smooth.

4. Add in the butter, sautéed garlic, nutritional yeast, cream cheese, salt, and pepper. Blend until creamy.

5. Top with another pinch of salt and pepper. Serve immediately.

BUTTERNUT AND GRAINS

SERVES: 6-8 // TOTAL TIME: 1 hour

This side dish is colorful and full of flavor. It's packed with healthy veggies and seeds. Feel free to sub in a different grain; I also like wild rice. Cook it according to package directions, using broth instead of water.

1 large butternut squash, peeled

2 Tablespoons avocado or grapeseed oil

¼ cup raw pumpkin seeds

2 cups chicken stock

1 cup quinoa

2 cups chopped kale leaves, washed and dried

½ white onion, chopped

4 cloves garlic, minced

Himalayan salt and freshly ground black pepper, to taste

1 Tablespoon nutritional yeast (optional)

1. Preheat the oven to 400°F and line a baking sheet with reusable parchment paper.

2. Cut squash in half lengthwise, clean out and discard the seeds in your compost bin or trash can. Place squash cut sides up on the baking sheet. Drizzle with 1 Tablespoon avocado or grapeseed oil, then place them face down on the baking sheet. Bake for about 40 minutes, or until fork-tender. Let cool, then cut into cubes.

3. Meanwhile, in a small, dry skillet over medium-low heat, toast the pumpkin seeds until golden brown, stirring frequently to keep from burning. Remove from pan and set aside.

4. Bring the chicken stock to a boil in a small saucepan; add quinoa. Reduce temperature and let simmer, covered, for 15–20 minutes, or until all of the liquid is absorbed.

5. Heat the remaining 1 Tablespoon avocado or grapeseed oil in a large skillet over medium-high heat, and sauté the kale, onion, and garlic until kale is slightly softened, about 4 minutes, tossing frequently with tongs.

6. Add the cubed squash and quinoa to the skillet and let cook for another 2–3 minutes. Remove from heat, place into a serving bowl and top with toasted pumpkin seeds. Season with salt and pepper and top with nutritional yeast, if desired, to add a cheesy flavor.

OVEN-ROASTED CARROTS

SERVES: 4 // TOTAL TIME: 40 minutes

Carrots are delicious pretty much any way you can eat them. I love to eat them raw and dip them in my vegan ranch, and I juice them often. These roasted carrots are super flavorful and pair well with any meat.

8 large carrots, peeled

2 Tablespoons avocado or grapeseed oil

Himalayan salt and freshly ground black pepper, to taste

⅓ cup raw pumpkin seeds

¼ cup pomegranate seeds

Yogurt Sauce

1 cup unsweetened coconut yogurt or dairy-free yogurt of choice

2 cloves garlic, minced

¼ cup tahini

1 Tablespoon freshly squeezed lemon juice

½ teaspoon ground cumin

1 Tablespoon local, raw honey

Filtered water, as needed

1. Preheat oven to 375°F and line a baking sheet with reusable parchment paper.

2. Place the carrots on the baking sheet, drizzle them with avocado or grapeseed oil, sprinkle with salt and pepper, and place in the oven. Roast for 30 minutes, or until the carrots are fork-tender.

3. Meanwhile, make the sauce: In a food processor or blender, blend all of the sauce ingredients together on high until smooth, scraping down the edges as necessary. If you prefer a thinner consistency add 1 Tablespoon of water at a time until you reach your desired consistency.

4. In a small, dry skillet over medium-low heat, toast the pumpkin seeds until golden brown, stirring frequently to keep from burning. Remove from pan and set aside.

5. Serve the carrots drizzled with the yogurt sauce and sprinkled with toasted pumpkin and pomegranate seeds.

ASIAN SLAW

SERVES: 4-6 // TOTAL TIME: 20 minutes

Growing up in Texas, where BBQ is on every corner, I ate a lot of coleslaw. This recipe puts a fun Asian twist on plain ole Texas coleslaw. Peaches are great here, but when not in season they're hard to find. If that is the case, you can use persimmon. Powdered miso soup can be found in the Asian section of the grocery store. You can also add some grilled chicken or shrimp to this slaw to give it an extra boost of protein.

¼ cup raw pumpkin seeds

1 Tablespoon avocado or grapeseed oil

2 poblano peppers, sliced

5 cups red or green cabbage, thinly sliced

2 carrots, peeled and shredded

½ white onion, sliced thin

½ cup loosely packed basil leaves

¼ cup loosely packed mint leaves

2 ripe peaches or persimmons, cut into chunks

1 firm, ripe avocado, peeled, pitted and sliced thin

2 Thai chiles, chopped (very spicy!)

Dressing

¼ cup cashew butter (pg. 196) or organic peanut butter

2 Tablespoons powdered white miso soup

2 Tablespoons freshly squeezed lime juice

1 teaspoon non-toasted sesame oil

1 teaspoon grated fresh ginger

4–5 Tablespoons filtered water, as needed

1. Make the dressing: In a small bowl, whisk together the cashew or peanut butter, miso soup powder, lime juice, sesame oil, and ginger. Whisk in the water 1 Tablespoon at a time until you get a consistency that you're able to drizzle. Set aside.

2. In a small, dry skillet over medium-low heat, toast the pumpkin seeds until golden brown, stirring frequently to keep from burning. Remove from pan and set aside.

3. Place the avocado or grapeseed oil and the poblanos in the same skillet, and sauté the poblanos for about 3–4 minutes, or until slightly tender.

4. In a large bowl, combine the poblanos, cabbage, carrots, onion, basil, mint, and ¾ of the dressing. Toss until well combined.

5. Serve topped with toasted pumpkin seeds, peaches, and avocado. If you would like to add some extra spice, top with Thai chiles. Put the rest of the dressing on the table for serving.

SWEET PLANTAINS

SERVES: 4 // TOTAL TIME: 10 minutes

Is this a side or a dessert? I had a hard time placing this one, because it can be either. I first tried these in Costa Rica back in 2013. I visited a small restaurant in Manuel Antonio, and these were served with my dish. I then ordered them with every meal for the rest of the trip. It wasn't until years later that I figured out how to cook them. These are a delicious, sweet treat that the whole family will love.

Tip: When you're buying plantains, make sure you get ones that look bruised and brown, like a banana that is going bad. Those are going to be the ones that are the sweetest.

3 ripe plantains

2 Tablespoons avocado or grapeseed oil

2 Tablespoons Kerrygold or dairy-free butter

2 Tablespoons brown or turbinado sugar

½ teaspoon ground cinnamon

Local, raw honey, for topping

1. Cut off the ends of the plantains and make a slit lengthwise just deep enough to pierce the peel. Remove the peel and discard into your compost bin or trash can. Cut the plantains into 1-inch-thick, angled slices.

2. In a skillet over medium heat, heat the oil and butter. Once the butter is melted, add the plantains and cook for about 90 seconds or until golden brown. Flip and sprinkle with sugar and cinnamon. Turn the heat to low, cover, and let simmer for 3–5 minutes or until tender and caramelized, stirring occasionally. Serve immediately.

SAUTÉED ASPARAGUS

SERVES: 4-6 // TOTAL TIME: 10 minutes

I love a good, crunchy asparagus. This side can be whipped up in a matter of minutes and pairs well with any meat, or seafood. They're best served right off the skillet.

1 medium-size bunch asparagus, washed

1 Tablespoon Kerrygold or dairy-free butter

Juice of 1 lemon

½ teaspoon garlic salt

½ teaspoon freshly ground black pepper

Lemon wedges, for garnish

1. Cut the bottom 2 inches of the asparagus off and discard into your compost bin or trash can.

2. In a large skillet over medium heat, melt the butter. Add the asparagus, lemon juice, garlic salt, and pepper. Sauté for about 3–4 minutes, tossing occasionally with tongs.

3. Serve immediately, garnished with lemon wedges.

SAUTÉED CHARD

SERVES: 2 // TOTAL TIME: 5 minutes

Chard grows like a weed in our garden. We sometimes get chard leaves that are well over a foot long and stalks that get up to 3 feet tall. I have such a surplus that I am giving it away all the time. I use it in salad, shakes, and sides—pretty much anything I can think of. This is a quick and easy way to sauté them up; you can serve them with any protein.

1 large bunch Swiss chard

1 Tablespoon avocado or grapeseed oil

¼ teaspoon garlic salt

1 clove garlic, sliced

1. Wash the chard and cut out the ribs. Discard into your compost bin or trash can. Pat dry with a paper towel and cut the leaves into manageable chunks.

2. In a large skillet over medium heat, add the chard and drizzle the avocado or grapeseed oil over the top. Add the garlic salt and sliced garlic; toss with tongs to combine. Sauté, tossing occasionally, for about 5 minutes, or until the chard is wilted and tender.

3. Serve immediately

DIPS, DRESSINGS, & SAUCES

RANCH DIP

MAKES: 1 ¾ cup   //   TOTAL TIME: 5 minutes

This vegan ranch dip has saved my life. When I first went dairy-free, giving up cheese and ranch nearly killed me. I experimented with a lot of products and made some really terrible ranch, but I didn't give up. The secret to this ranch dip is the brand of milk-free sour cream. Tofutti can be found at any health food store like Sprouts, Whole Foods, etc.

1 (12-oz) container Tofutti milk-free sour cream

3-4 Tablespoons ranch seasoning (Hidden Valley)

2 Tablespoons filtered water, plus more as needed

1–2 Tablespoons sriracha (optional)

In a small bowl, whisk the sour cream, ranch seasoning, and 1 Tablespoon of water together. If you want a thinner consistency, add more water, 1 Tablespoon at a time, whisking until you have your desired consistency. You can add more ranch seasoning if you would like to make it more flavorful. This will keep in the fridge in an airtight container for up to 5 days.

Tip: For spicy ranch, add in the sriracha.

HOT HONEY SAUCE

MAKES: ⅓ cup // TOTAL TIME: 10 minutes

This dipping sauce is seriously addictive. I taste-test it way too many times before serving it. It reminds me of the flavor of the honey butter biscuit from Chick-fil-A, but with an extra kick of spice. This is a must for dipping coconut shrimp and chicken tenders.

2 Tablespoons Kerrygold or dairy-free butter

¼ cup local, raw honey

1-2 Tablespoon cayenne pepper, depending your spice tolerance

1. Soften the butter in the microwave in a glass bowl for about 20 seconds; you want it to be almost all the way melted.

2. Add in the honey and cayenne. Whisk together until well combined. This will keep in the fridge in an airtight container for up to 5 days.

HONEY MUSTARD

MAKES: 1 cup // TOTAL TIME: 10 minutes

I love mustard, all kinds of mustard. I could eat it on almost anything. Adding honey into mustard has to be one of the best ideas ever! This sauce is great to have around the house for the kids to dip their tenders in or to put on a burger. The best thing about it is it's super easy to make. You can use any kind of mustard—yellow, stone-ground, or Dijon—as a base and just whisk in some honey and you're done! I quit buying most store-bought condiments and dressings when I realized how much unnecessary crap was in them; instead I like to make my own. It's much healthier!

¾ cup mustard of choice: stone-ground, yellow, or Dijon

¼ cup local, raw honey

Whisk the ingredients together in a small bowl. This will keep in the fridge in an airtight container for up to 5 days.

PECAN PESTO

MAKES: 1 cup // TOTAL TIME: 5 minutes

My husband loves pesto, and when we cut out dairy, it was one of the things that got the boot. By replacing Parmesan cheese with nutritional yeast, this pesto becomes dairy-free. We love it with chicken, pasta, or veggies.

½ cup raw pecans

2 cups packed basil leaves

⅓ cup avocado or grapeseed oil

4 cloves garlic, minced

1 Tablespoon nutritional yeast

⅛ teaspoon garlic salt

1. In a small, dry skillet over medium-low heat, toast the pecans until golden brown, stirring frequently to keep from burning. Remove from pan and set aside.

2. Place toasted pecans and remaining ingredients into a food processor or blender. Blend on high until well combined, scraping down the sides when necessary. This will keep in the fridge in an airtight container for 3-4 days, but it's best served fresh.

STIR-FRY SAUCE

MAKES: 1 cup // TOTAL TIME: 5 minutes

If you can't tell from the recipes in this book, I love Asian food. When you are gluten-free, Asian restaurants are pretty much off-limits. Anything that has soy sauce in it, which is everything, contains gluten. But using tamari or liquid aminos in place of soy sauce has made eating Asian food possible again. I love to use Mason jars for making sauces. It's easy to just screw the lid on and shake to mix as well as to store any leftovers in the fridge. Fewer dishes mean more time to do fun things. But if you don't have a Mason jar, just whisk them together in a small bowl.

Tip: You can heat the honey up for about 15 seconds to soften it to make it easier to mix in.

½ cup tamari or any gluten-free soy sauce

½ cup chicken stock

1 Tablespoon local, raw honey

4 cloves garlic, minced

2-inch piece of ginger, peeled and grated

1 Tablespoon non-toasted sesame oil

1 teaspoon rice vinegar

Place all ingredients in a Mason jar or small bowl and shake or whisk until well combined. This will keep in an airtight container for up to 5 days in the fridge.

EASY GUACAMOLE

MAKES: 2 cups // TOTAL TIME: 5 minutes

I've been making this simple, 3 ingredient guacamole for years. I always get compliments on it when I have people over. When I make my guacamole, it always has lots of garlic and lemon. If you want an extra kick, you can spice it up with chopped jalapeños or habaneros.

Tip: You can try subbing in orange juice for the lemon juice for an equally great and fun twist.

3 large, ripe avocados

¼ cup freshly squeezed lemon juice

1 Tablespoon garlic salt

Chopped jalapeño or habanero peppers (optional)

1. Cut the avocados in half and remove the pits and skin. Use a fork to mash up the avocado to your desired chunkiness.

2. Mix in the lemon juice and garlic salt, stirring to combine.

3. Add chopped jalapeños or habaneros, if desired. This will keep in the fridge in an airtight container for 2–3 days, but it's best served fresh.

EDAMAME GUACAMOLE

MAKES: 2 cups // TOTAL TIME: 5 minutes

Asian meets Mexican? Yes, please. This adds a fresh twist on guacamole, and I love it. Make sure to buy frozen shelled edamame and let them thaw before blending. This guacamole can be used for dipping veggies or chips, on avocado toast, on a burger, and so many other ways.

1 cup frozen shelled edamame, thawed

2 firm, ripe avocados, peeled and pitted

3 cloves garlic

¼ white onion

2 jalapeño peppers, cut in half

Juice of 2 limes

1 teaspoon garlic salt

Freshly ground black pepper, to taste

2 Tablespoons filtered water

Tortilla chips and/or veggies, for serving

1. In a food processor or blender, combine edamame, avocados, garlic, onion, jalapeños, lime juice, garlic salt, and pepper. Blend on high until well combined, scraping down the edges as necessary. Add in the water and pulse until creamy and smooth.

2. Transfer to a serving bowl and serve with chips or veggies. This will keep in the fridge in an airtight container for 2-3 days, but it's best served fresh.

175

THE BEST FRESH SALSA

MAKES: 2 cups // TOTAL TIME: 5 minutes

I make this salsa several times a week. I love my salsa spicy, but there is an option here to make it mild as well. I use all fresh ingredients and make it right before I serve it. You basically just toss everything into a food processor and pulse it until it's your desired consistency.

2 cups red and yellow cherry tomatoes

¼ white onion

3 large jalapeño peppers, cut in half

4–5 cloves garlic

½ teaspoon ground cumin

½ teaspoon garlic salt

1 habanero or ghost pepper (optional)

Place all ingredients into the food processor or blender and pulse until you get your desired chunkiness. This will keep in the fridge in an airtight container for up to 5 days, but it tastes so much better fresh.

Tip: Don't put your tomatoes in the fridge, it takes away the flavor. Keep them on your counter or in your pantry.

PINEAPPLE PICO DE GALLO

MAKES: about 4 cups // TOTAL TIME: 10 minutes

This is a sweet spin on pico de gallo. I love the sweetness of the pineapple with the tang of the lime and the spice of the jalapeño. It makes the perfect chip dip or topper for tacos.

Tip: Sub mangoes in for the pineapple for a fun twist.

1 small pineapple, peeled, cored, and chopped into ½-inch cubes

4 jalapeño peppers, chopped small

½ white onion, chopped small

2 cups cherry tomatoes, quartered

1 teaspoon garlic salt

½ teaspoon ground cumin

1 teaspoon onion powder

Juice of 2 limes

Tortilla chips, for serving

Mix all ingredients together in a bowl, and serve with tortilla chips. This will keep in the fridge in an airtight container for up to 3 days, but it's best served fresh.

FRESH TOMATILLO SALSA

MAKES: 2 cups // TOTAL TIME: 5 minutes

All my life, I never knew what the heck was in green salsa. It wasn't until my thirties, when I planted a tomatillo plant, harvested a ton, and didn't know what to do with them that I figured it out. I googled it, and salsa verde it was! This salsa tastes so fresh and delicious. All ingredients can be thrown in a food processor raw and ready to go in about five minutes. It's great for tacos or just for dippin' chips. If you add in the pineapple, it gives the salsa a sweet-tangy kick.

10 tomatillos, husks removed, cut in half

¼ white onion

2–3 jalapeño peppers, cut in half

3 cloves garlic

Juice of 1 lime

½ teaspoon ground cumin

1 teaspoon garlic salt

1 habanero pepper (optional)

1 cup chopped fresh pineapple (optional)

Put all of the ingredients into the food processor or blender and blend on high until well combined, about 30 seconds. This will keep in the fridge in an airtight container for up to 5 days, but it's best served fresh.

SPICY MANGO SALSA

MAKES: 2 cups // TOTAL TIME: 25 minutes

I don't know about you, but when I go to Mexico, one of my favorite street treats to get is a mango with Tajín on it. Tajín is a yummy chili-lime seasoning that makes my mouth water while I'm thinking about it. Eating spicy mangoes while lying on the beach is something I dream about. This salsa is a play on spicy mangoes. It tastes great on just about anything!

1 large mango, peeled and sliced

3 habanero peppers

½ white onion

4 cloves garlic

¼ cup apple cider vinegar

2 Tablespoons local, raw honey

½ teaspoon ground cumin

½ teaspoon allspice

1 teaspoon ginger powder

1 teaspoon sea salt

1. Add all ingredients in a food processor or blender and blend on high until smooth.

2. Transfer into a saucepan and bring to a boil over medium-high heat. Reduce heat and simmer for 10 minutes, stirring occasionally.

3. Let cool completely before serving. This will keep in the fridge in an airtight container for up to 5 days, but it's best served fresh.

BABA GANOUSH

MAKES: 2 cups // TOTAL TIME: 50 minutes

My husband and I traveled to Turkey a few years back on our honeymoon and had such an amazing time. Neither one of us drink, so we love to go restaurant-hopping instead of bar hopping. The food in Turkey is amazing, and I couldn't seem to get enough of the baba ganoush. I am not a fan of eggplant, but for some reason I love this dish. When we got home, I played around with the recipe until I came up with one that I loved. Now you can enjoy it too!

2 large eggplants

½ cup tahini

4 cloves garlic

⅓ cup freshly squeezed lemon juice

½ teaspoon ground cumin, plus more for garnish

Pinch of Himalayan salt

Pinch of freshly ground black pepper

2 Tablespoons extra-virgin olive oil, plus more for garnish

2 Tablespoons chopped fresh flat-leaf parsley, plus more for garnish

¼ cup kalamata olives, for garnish (optional)

Sprinkle of paprika, for garnish

1. Preheat the oven to 400°F and line a baking sheet with reusable parchment paper.

2. Wash and dry the eggplants. Pierce the skin all over several times with a fork, and evenly char the whole eggplants directly on a gas stove flame or under a broiler, turning the eggplant as needed. This takes about 8 minutes.

3. Place charred eggplants on the baking sheet and roast for 30 minutes, or until tender. Remove from the oven and let cool.

4. Cut the eggplants in half lengthwise, and scrape out the insides with a spoon. Place eggplant flesh and the rest of the remaining ingredients (excluding the garnishes) into a food processor or blender and blend on high until well combined.

5. Pour mixture into a bowl, and garnish the dip with a drizzle of olive oil, chopped parsley, olives (if using), and a sprinkle of paprika. This will keep in the fridge in an airtight container for up to 5 days, but it's best served fresh.

DILL & BASIL HUMMUS

MAKES: 2 cups // TOTAL TIME: 10 minutes

I use basil all the time, but dill is one of those herbs that sits in my garden often untouched. I just don't know much to do with it other than make egg salad or pickles, which I have yet to master. One day I started experimenting with hummus, and I came up with this delicious recipe. I love to have hummus on hand to eat with gluten-free pita chips or veggies.

1 (15.5-oz) can garbanzo beans, drained and rinsed

¼ cup freshly squeezed lemon juice

1 Tablespoon extra-virgin olive oil, plus more for garnish

1 Tablespoon flaxseed oil

¼ cup tahini

2 Tablespoons tamari

3 cloves garlic, minced

2 Tablespoons chopped fresh dill, plus more for garnish

4 large basil leaves, plus more for garnish

Gluten-free pita chips, for dippin' (optional)

Veggies, for dippin' (optional)

1. Combine all of the ingredients (excluding garnishes, chips, and veggies) in a food processor or blender. Blend on high until smooth, about 1 minute, scraping down the edges as necessary. If you want a thinner consistency, add 1 Tablespoon water at a time until it reaches your desired consistency.

2. Serve garnished with dill, basil, and a drizzle of olive oil on top. Serve with gluten-free pita chips or veggies for dippin'. This will keep in the fridge in an airtight container for up to 5 days, but it's best served fresh.

CASHEW QUESO

MAKES: 1 cups // TOTAL TIME: 10 minutes

I am the kind of person who doesn't like to have more than one or two of any one thing at a time. I am very organized and hate clutter. My husband knows this, and when I mentioned to him that we were running low on cashews, he ordered fourteen 2-lb bags of cashews on Amazon. When they arrived, he couldn't quit laughing. I had cashews stuffed in every corner of my kitchen and pantry for a few weeks before I began to figure out what the heck to make with them all. Making cashew queso came as a recommendation from a friend when I posted on Instagram a photo of the massive amounts of cashews everywhere. My journey to using all of these cashews led to this yummy treat.

¾ cup hot, filtered water, plus more as needed

1 cup raw cashews

2 cloves garlic

2 Tablespoons nutritional yeast, plus more for garnish

½ teaspoon ground cumin

1 teaspoon chili powder

½ teaspoon Himalayan salt

1 teaspoon cayenne pepper (optional)

1 teaspoon sriracha (optional)

Tortilla chips, for serving

1. Add all ingredients into a food processor or blender. Blend on high until smooth, about 30 seconds. If you would like a thinner consistency, add 1 more Tablespoon of hot water at a time until you get your desired consistency.

2. Top with a sprinkle of nutritional yeast and serve with chips. This will keep in the fridge in an airtight container for 3–4 days, but it's best served fresh. Reheat in a small saucepan over low heat.

Homemade Vinaigrettes

Almost all store-bought salad dressings are packed with unnecessary crap. Several years ago, I threw out all of my store-bought dressings and started making my own. I like to use avocado or grapeseed oil in dressings because it tastes lighter and nuttier, but you can use olive oil as well for any of these dressings.

WATERMELON VINAIGRETTE

MAKES: 1 ½ cups // TOTAL TIME: 10 minutes

2 cups cubed watermelon

¼ cup local, raw honey

1 Tablespoon apple cider vinegar

1 Tablespoon Dijon mustard

1 teaspoon Himalayan salt

½ cup avocado or grapeseed oil

In a food processor or blender, combine the watermelon, honey, apple cider vinegar, Dijon mustard, and salt. Blend on high until well combined and smooth. Turn to low, and slowly add in the avocado or grapeseed oil, blending until emulsified. This will keep in the fridge in an airtight container for up to 5 days, but it's best served fresh.

STRAWBERRY VINAIGRETTE

MAKES: 1 ½ cups // TOTAL TIME: 10 minutes

1 cup fresh strawberries

1 teaspoon apple cider vinegar

1 Tablespoon local, raw honey

¼ teaspoon Himalayan salt

¼ teaspoon freshly ground black pepper

½ cup avocado or grapeseed oil

In a food processor or blender, combine the strawberries, apple cider vinegar, honey, salt, and pepper. Blend on high until well combined and smooth. Turn to low, and slowly add in the avocado or grapeseed oil, blending until emulsified. This will keep in the fridge in an airtight container for up to 5 days, but it's best served fresh.

CHAMPAGNE VINAIGRETTE

MAKES: 1 ½ cups // TOTAL TIME: 10 minutes

½ cup avocado or grapeseed oil

¼ cup champagne or white wine vinegar

Juice of 1 lemon

1 Tablespoon Dijon mustard

1 Tablespoon local, raw honey

3 cloves garlic, minced

1 teaspoon cracked red pepper

Mix all ingredients together in a Mason jar or a bowl, and shake or whisk until well combined. This will keep in the fridge in an airtight container for up to 5 days, but it's best served fresh.

RASPBERRY VINAIGRETTE

MAKES: 1 ½ cups // TOTAL TIME: 10 minutes

1 cup fresh raspberries

1 teaspoon white wine vinegar

1 Tablespoon local, raw honey

1 small shallot

¼ teaspoon Himalayan salt

½ cup avocado or grapeseed oil

In a food processor or blender, combine raspberries, white wine vinegar, honey, shallot and salt. Blend high until well combined and smooth. Turn to low, and slowly add in the avocado or grapeseed oil, blending until emulsified. This will keep in the fridge in an airtight container for up to 5 days, but it's best served fresh.

STAPLES

Homemade Milks

Have you ever looked at the ingredients on a box of store-bought nut milk? There are guaranteed to be ingredients that you can't pronounce or don't know what they are. That, along with how many boxes I was recycling per month, inspired me to start making my own. With just a few simple, all-natural ingredients, you too can make your own. This is something that I do every few days. My husband and I drink protein shakes every morning, and when we have the kids they do too, so we go through a lot of nut milk. I store our nut milk in large glass containers with airtight lids in the fridge. Large Mason jars also work great. I usually make four servings of milk at a time so I can go several days without having to remake.

Tip: Add a couple Tablespoons of cacao to any milk to make it chocolate.

ALMOND MILK

MAKES: 5 cups // TOTAL TIME: 15 minutes (plus overnight soaking)

Making almond milk can seem time-consuming, but it's really not. All you need is a high-speed blender. I recommend getting a Vitamix, as it does a lot of the work for you. You will need a nut bag or cheesecloth (I prefer to use a nut bag) to strain out the pulp. You can also purchase an Almond Cow, which has a built-in strainer for the milk, but this is not necessary.

1 cup raw almonds

4 cups filtered water

1 large Medjool date, pitted

1 Tablespoon vanilla extract (optional)

½ teaspoon Himalayan salt

1. Soak the almonds overnight in the fridge. Drain and rinse them well.

2. Place all of the ingredients into a high-speed blender, and blend on high for 2 minutes.

3. Use a nut bag to strain out the pulp and discard into your compost bin or trash can. Store the nut milk in the fridge; it will last 5–7 days in an airtight container.

CASHEW MILK

MAKES: 5 cups // TOTAL TIME: 10 minutes

Cashew milk is my favorite milk, so it gets made very often at our house. Unlike the almond milk process, you will not need to soak cashews overnight or, if you're using a high-speed blender like a Vitamix, strain it. Just throw everything in, blend it, pour it into glass containers, and it's good to go. If you're using a blender that leaves you with thick, pulpy cashew milk, you will need to strain it through a nut bag before storing in the fridge.

1 cup raw cashews

4 cups filtered water

1 large Medjool date, pitted

1 Tablespoon vanilla extract (optional)

½ teaspoon Himalayan salt

Place all of the ingredients into a high-speed blender. Blend on high for 2 minutes. Strain through a nut bag if necessary. Store the nut milk in the fridge; it will last 5–7 days in an airtight container.

WALNUT MILK

MAKES: 5 cups // TOTAL TIME: 15 minutes (plus overnight soaking)

Walnut milk is not as popular as the other nut milks, but it's just as delicious, if not more. It's creamy and smooth and is high in omega-3s. You'll need to strain the pulp out through a nut bag or cheesecloth after blending.

1 cup raw walnuts

4 cups filtered water

1 large Medjool date, pitted

1 Tablespoon vanilla extract (optional)

½ teaspoon Himalayan salt

1. Soak the walnuts overnight in the fridge. Drain and rinse them well.

2. Place all of the ingredients into a high-speed blender, and blend on high for 2 minutes.

3. Use a nut bag to strain out the pulp and discard into your compost bin or trash can. Store the nut milk in the fridge; it will last 5–7 days in an airtight container.

CASSAVA FLOUR TORTILLAS

MAKES: 8 tortillas // TOTAL TIME: 20 minutes

The first time I ever tried cassava flour tortillas was in Cabo San Lucas, Mexico. My husband and I were eating at Toro, and we ordered some amazing soft-shell crab tacos. Unlike most gluten-free tortillas, these were stretchy and never broke apart. I asked the server what the tortilla was made of, and it was cassava flour. It wasn't until a year and a half later that I finally tried to make them at home. They're the BEST tortillas I've ever had, and they're super easy. My husband has now taken over the tortilla-making in our house, and he might be better at it than me. You just need a tortilla press and some reusable parchment paper to make them. I use ghee, which is free of casein and lactose, but if you're not able to have ghee, you can sub it out for palm shortening.

Tip: Having a tortilla warmer to store the tortillas from the time they're cooked to the time they get eaten is very important; it softens them a bit. You can improvise by covering them with a damp dish towel.

1 cup cassava flour

¼ teaspoon flaky sea salt

1 teaspoon baking soda

1 teaspoon cream of tartar

1 Tablespoon ghee

1 Tablespoon MCT oil, ghee, or palm shortening

⅔ cup hot, filtered water

1. Heat up a griddle or pan over medium-high heat.

2. Whisk together all of the dry ingredients in a bowl. Add in the ghee and the MCT oil. Mix until well combined.

3. Add in the hot water and stir with a spoon until it has formed a dough. Use your hands and form into a ball. Knead the dough for a few minutes until well combined. Roll into 1-inch balls. Using a tortilla press with reusable parchment paper on each side, press firmly to flatten each ball. Remove from the parchment paper and place the tortilla on the hot griddle or pan.

4. Cook for about 1–2 minutes on each side. The tortilla will go from being almost transparent to off-white with some brown spots.

5. Repeat this process with all of the tortillas, making sure to store them in the warmer when they get pulled off the stove (this softens them). If cooking on a griddle or a large skillet, you can do multiple tortillas at a time. The tortillas can be stored in the fridge in an airtight container for 5–7 days and reheated.

CASHEW BUTTER

MAKES: 2 cups // TOTAL TIME: 10 minutes

Cashew butter has become my favorite nut butter. I always have it on hand in the pantry to make butter cups, to serve with apples to the kids, or just to eat a spoonful. Buying cashew butter at the store can be really expensive—around $15 for a 14-oz jar. Making your own is simple and surprisingly less expensive.

2 cups raw cashews

3 Tablespoons avocado or grapeseed oil, or more as needed

1. Place all of the ingredients into a food processor and blend on high, scraping down the sides as necessary, until smooth. If you would like a creamier consistency, you can add 1 more tablespoon of oil at a time until you reach your desired consistency.

2. Cashew butter can be stored in a Mason jar or airtight container in the pantry for up to 6 months.

ALMOND BUTTER

MAKES: 2 cups // TOTAL TIME: 10 minutes

We always have almond butter in the pantry. I make a large batch and store it in a Mason jar. It comes in handy when the kids need a quick snack or for some of the dessert or protein-ball recipes.

1 cup raw almonds

3 Tablespoons avocado or grapeseed oil, or more as needed

1. Place all of the ingredients into a food processor and blend on high, scraping down the sides as necessary, until smooth. If you would like a creamier consistency, you can add 1 more tablespoon of oil at a time until you reach your desired consistency.

2. Almond butter can be stored in a Mason jar or airtight container in the pantry for up to 6 months.

ZOODLES & BUOODLES

MAKES: 4-6 servings // TOTAL TIME: 10 minutes

Veggie noodles are a life-saver in the gluten-free world. They're so easy, too! Once you spiralize them, you're pretty much done. When I use them for spaghetti, I pour the sauce over the noodles and the heat of the sauce slightly cooks the noodles to perfection. There are tons of spiralizers on the market. Handheld ones are great if you're using zucchinis, but you will need a more heavy-duty one for butternut squash.

4 large zucchinis or 1 large butternut, peeled

1. Zucchini: Wash and dry the zucchinis, and cut off the ends.
Butternut squash: Cut off the bulbous, seeded side of the squash, and reserve for another use. Peel the neck of the squash.

2. Using a spiralizer, place the zucchini or butternut firmly in and turn the handle to create spirals. You may also use a mandoline slicer with the julienne attachment. I like mine spiralized thick, but you can do any size. If you're not using them right away, you can store them in your fridge in an airtight container for 2–3 days.

DRINKS

CELERY JUICE

MAKES: 16 ounces // TOTAL TIME: 5 minutes

Juicing celery has become a daily ritual in our house. Drinking 16 ounces of celery juice first thing in the morning on an empty stomach, then waiting 30 minutes before eating, kick-starts your digestive system, helps clear up complexion, and acts as an anti-inflammatory. A cold press juicer is slower and yields more juice than a normal juicer, but you can use any kind of juicer you like or even a blender and strain it out with a nut bag. You gain the most benefits by drinking it immediately after it's juiced.

Tip: A little time-saving tip is to buy pre-cut celery packs from Costco. Each bag makes thirty-two ounces in my cold press juicer, which is the perfect amount for both of us each morning.

1 stalk of celery, top and bottoms trimmed

Feed the celery through the juicer. If you do not have a juicer, you can use a high-speed blender. You will need to strain out the pulp with a nut bag or cheesecloth. Drink immediately. If you're not able to drink it immediately, you can store it in the fridge in a Mason jar or airtight container for up to 24 hours.

BERRY SODA

MAKES: 2 servings // TOTAL TIME: 10 minutes

I don't buy soda. It's full of sugar, and if it's in the fridge, I will drink it—lots of it. My favorite is a good, ice-cold Dr. Pepper, and anytime I go to my dad's house to visit, I always drink one while eating popcorn at night. Now I am not saying this will replace an ice-cold Dr. Pepper, but it will get you your fizzy fix.

4 strawberries, sliced, plus more for garnish

½ cup blueberries, plus more for garnish

1 Tablespoon local, raw honey

1 Tablespoon freshly squeezed orange juice

Crushed ice

16 oz sparkling water (Topo Chico)

1. In a metal shaker, muddle the fruit with the honey and orange juice until well combined.

2. Split the fruit mixture between two glasses. Fill to the top with crushed ice and top with sparkling water. Give it a gentle stir, being careful not to make it flat. Garnish with blueberries and strawberries.

CHARCOAL LIME/LEMONADE

MAKES: 1 serving // TOTAL TIME: 10 minutes

I discovered this drink at a restaurant in Austin. I watched as the server kept bringing out these black drinks garnished so beautifully with lemons and mint. I, of course, had to order one. The color may not look appealing, but it's full of flavor. Charcoal aids in removing toxins, bacteria, and gas from your body while keeping you hydrated. Kids love this drink. It's really fun to make with them too! Topo Chico is my favorite sparkling water to use because it gives you the best fizz.

1 capsule coconut charcoal

Juice of 1 lemon or 2 limes

2 Tablespoons local, raw honey

Crushed ice

8 oz sparkling water (Topo Chico)

Lemon or lime slice, for garnish

1. Open the coconut charcoal capsule and pour the powder into a small bowl. Discard the capsule. Add the lemon or lime juice and honey, and whisk until well combined.

2. Fill a glass with crushed ice and pour in the charcoal-citrus mixture. Fill to the top with sparkling water, and give it a gentle stir, being careful to not make it flat. Garnish with a slice of lemon or lime.

MOJITO MOCKTAIL

MAKES: 2 servings // TOTAL TIME: 10 minutes

This is the mocktail of all mocktails. It's so delicious, you will think you're sitting on a beach sippin' a mojito. It's light, refreshing, and perfect for any sunny day. If you want to enjoy this drink frozen, just add 1 ½ cups of ice to the blender along with the ingredients and voilà, you have yourself a tasty frozen mocktail. Of course, you're more than welcome to add rum if you're trying to get a little tipsy!

½ cup freshly squeezed lemon juice

1 teaspoon grated fresh ginger

10 mint leaves, plus more for garnish

1 cup coconut water

1 cup filtered water

2 Tablespoons local, raw honey

Lemon slices, for garnish

Crushed ice

1. Combine all ingredients (except lemon slices and ice) in a blender. Blend on high until well combined.

2. Pour over glasses of crushed ice. Garnish each with a mint spring and a lemon slice.

3. If you would like to make frozen mocktails, add two glasses full of ice to the blender, and blend until well combined.

WATERMELON AGUA FRESCA

MAKES: 4 servings // TOTAL TIME: 15 minutes

I don't know about you guys, but I love to go to the Mexican market and get an agua fresca. They're so refreshing and delicious. They're made simply from fruit, water, lime juice, and a little natural sweetener, which makes it super refreshing and doesn't give you a sugar overload.

2 cups diced watermelon, plus more for garnish

½ cup filtered water

3 basil leaves, plus more for garnish

2 Tablespoons local, raw honey

Juice of 1 lime

Crushed ice

4 lime slices

1. Place watermelon, water, 3 basil leaves, honey, and lemon juice into a blender, and blend on high until well combined, about 30 seconds.

2. Pour over glasses full of crushed ice, and garnish each with a watermelon slice, a slice of lime, and a basil leaf.

CUCUMBER-BASIL FRESCA

MAKES: 2 servings // TOTAL TIME: 10 minutes

We found this amazing hotel on this little island off the coast of Cancun when we were on vacation. The cute beachfront restaurant had a large variety of wellness drinks and shots on the menu. We tried every drink they had on the menu. Adam fell in love with this basil drink and when we got back home, he kept asking me to recreate it. So here we have it, another refreshing drink.

4 large basil leaves, plus more for garnish

8 mint leaves

½ cup cucumber, peeled and chopped

½ Tablespoon local, raw honey

Juice of 2 limes

Crushed ice

16 oz sparkling water (Topo Chico)

2 cucumber slices, for garnish

1. Put the basil, mint, cucumber, honey, and lime juice into a blender and blend on high until fully combined, about 15 seconds.

2. Fill two glasses with crushed ice, pour the mixture into the glasses, and top with sparkling water. Give it a gentle stir, being careful not to make it flat.

3. Garnish each with a basil leaf and a cucumber slice.

TURMERIC ORANGE GODDESS

MAKES: 1 serving   //   TOTAL TIME: 5 minutes

Looking for a super delicious drink that has a ton of added health benefits? Turmeric is a powerful anti-inflammatory that helps aching joints, balances blood sugar, and aids in brighter, healthier skin. It's also said to help with arthritis and depression, as well as help prevent cancer and Alzheimer's disease. Needless to say, I love adding turmeric into my drinks in order to reap those amazing benefits. This beautiful orange drink is packed with healthy ingredients and tastes so good.

Juice of 2 oranges

Juice of 1 lime

1 Tablespoon local, raw honey

1 teaspoon grated fresh ginger

1 teaspoon grated fresh turmeric

Pinch of sea salt

Crushed ice

Orange slice, for garnish

1. Whisk together the orange juice, lime juice, honey, ginger, turmeric, and salt in a small bowl until well combined.

2. Pour over a glass of crushed ice and garnish with an orange slice.

Infused Waters

Infused waters are my jam. I make them every morning before I go work out. I fill a big water dispenser with ice, water, and whatever fruit I have on hand. When I get home, the water is cold, and the fruit has had time to infuse. All day I am able to pour myself a glass of flavorful water. Turmeric is a something that I always add to my water; it's a potent anti-inflammatory and antioxidant, and the sea salt and piperine help activate all of the benefits of the turmeric in your body.

TURMERIC-ORANGE WATER

MAKES: 8 cups // TOTAL TIME: 5 minutes

10 cups ice cubes

8 cups filtered water

2 oranges, sliced

⅛ teaspoon ground turmeric

⅛ teaspoon piperine

⅛ teaspoon Himalayan salt

Put all of the ingredients into the water dispenser and stir. Continue to add ice as the day goes on, so it stays cold.

STRAWBERRY-MINT WATER

MAKES: 8 cups // TOTAL TIME: 5 minutes

10 cups ice cubes

8 cups filtered water

15 strawberries, sliced

Handful of mint leaves

Put all of the ingredients into the water dispenser and stir. Continue to add ice as the day goes on, so it stays cold.

LEMON, MINT & BASIL WATER

MAKES: 8 cups // TOTAL TIME: 5 minutes

10 cups ice cubes

8 cups filtered water

2 lemons, sliced

1 small cucumber, sliced

Handful of mint leaves

Put all of the ingredients into the water dispenser and stir. Continue to add ice as the day goes on, so it stays cold.

GINGER, MINT & SPARKLING WATER

MAKES: 1 cup // TOTAL TIME: 5 minutes

1 cup crushed ice

5 mint leaves

1-inch piece of ginger, peeled and sliced

6 ounces sparkling water (Topo Chico)

Put all of the ingredients into a glass and gently stir. Let infuse for a few minutes before drinking. You can also make this into a large batch, but the sparkling water will get flat as the ice melts.

Infused Ice Cubes

These ice cubes are so great to have in your freezer. I've turned off my ice maker, and now I fill my ice cube tray with these awesome infused ice cubes. You can use these as a base in any drink. I usually add them to my sparkling water, but they're great in just about anything. These cubes are always a hit at parties, and the kids love them too. They like to take them straight out of the freezer and consider them a dessert—I consider that a WIN! These are super easy to make and last for about a month in the freezer. The best part about these ice cubes is that they don't water down your drink; they just add flavor. You can also freeze coffee and add those cubes to your iced coffee.

Tip: Buy a silicone ice tray on Amazon. The cubes pop right out.

LEMON-GINGER ICE CUBES

MAKES: 24 ice cubes // TOTAL TIME: 10 minutes (plus freezing)

Juice of 10 lemons

3-inch piece of ginger, peeled and sliced

1. Put the lemon juice into a silicone ice tray. Add the chopped ginger evenly into the trays.

2. Freeze overnight. Store in your freezer's ice maker, or just leave them in the silicone trays and pop them out when ready to use!

LIME-MINT ICE CUBES

MAKES: 24 ice cubes // TOTAL TIME: 10 minutes (plus freezing)

Juice of 15 limes

Grated zest of 3 limes

½ cup chopped fresh mint leaves

1. Put the lime juice into a silicone ice tray. Add the lime zest and mint leaves evenly into the trays.

2. Freeze overnight. Store in your freezer's ice maker, or just leave them in the silicone trays and pop out when ready to use!

WATERMELON-LIME ICE CUBES

MAKES: 24 ice cubes // TOTAL TIME: 10 minutes (plus freezing)

½ seedless watermelon

Juice of 3 limes

Grated zest of 2 limes

1. Cut the watermelon into chunks, and blend on high in a food processor or blender until smooth.

2. Add the lime juice and zest, and give it one more quick blend.

3. Pour into silicone ice trays, and freeze overnight. Store in your freezer's ice maker, or just leave them in the silicone trays and pop them out when ready to use!

Wellness Shots

Shots are usually what everyone on vacation is asking me to do, and I always turn them down. But not these shots! I can drink these all day long. Below are a few of my favorite wellness shots to make at home. They're quick, easy shots that are packed with health benefits and are super tasty.

THE REFRESHER SHOT

MAKES: 2 shots // TOTAL TIME: 10 minutes

I put my cold press juicer to work. I use it at least two times a day. This is my favorite concoction that comes out of the juicer. It's sweet and delicious. I love making a batch and pouring it into little shot-size Mason jars and storing them in the fridge. It's an easy grab-and-go when I need a little something sweet, plus it's packed with healthy benefits. Turmeric is a powerful anti-inflammatory and ginger is loaded with antioxidants that is said to help your body fight off chronic diseases, like high blood pressure and heart disease. It also promotes healthy aging.

2 carrots, peeled

2-inch piece of ginger, peeled

2-inch piece of turmeric, peeled

1 orange

1. In a juicer, juice the carrots, ginger, and turmeric. If you're using a blender, you will need to use a nut bag to strain out the pulp. Discard the pulp into your compost bin or trash can.

2. With a hand juicer, juice the orange.

3. Combine all of the juice together in a small bowl and whisk until well combined. Pour into 2 ounce mason jars or shot glasses. Can be stored in the fridge in an airtight container or mason jar for up to 5 days.

FLU REMEDY SHOT

MAKES: 2 shots // TOTAL TIME: 10 minutes

I experienced this delicious shot on a little island in Mexico. I don't drink, so I am always looking on the menu for fun non-alcoholic drinks. Usually I am disappointed by a very small selection, but at this restaurant they had some really cool, healthy drinks. I stayed on this island for only two nights, and I bet I ordered about six of these by the time I left. They're perfect if you have a sore throat or, as in my case, are just craving a delicious sweet treat. The ingredients add tons of health benefits including helping ease nausea, bloating, inflammation, and digestion problems. It can also help clear up your skin. Throw one back—I promise you will love it.

Tip: Add a dash of cayenne for a kick of spice.

¼ cup freshly squeezed lime or lemon juice

1 teaspoon freshly grated, peeled ginger

1 Tablespoon local, raw honey

Dash of cayenne (optional)

Whisk all ingredients together and pour into 2 ounce mason jars or shot glasses. Can be stored in the fridge in an airtight container or mason jar for up to 5 days.

JAMU WELLNESS SHOT

MAKES: 2 shots // TOTAL TIME: 10 minutes

I lived in Southeast Asia for a year when I was in my early 20s. Bali was one of my favorite stops. I love the culture, and the food there is amazing. There are those certain things—tastes or smells—that bring you back to a certain time in your past. This is one of them for me. It makes me think of riding a motorbike around the beach town of Canggu, barefoot, with salty hair, and in my bikini.

This little magical Balinese-inspired shot is a great anti-inflammatory. It is high in antioxidants and promotes good heart health, boosts your digestion and well-being all while being a natural detox for your liver and kidneys.

1-inch piece of fresh turmeric, peeled

1-inch piece of fresh ginger, peeled

1 orange

2 lemons

⅛ Tablespoon piperine

¼ teaspoon MCT oil

1 Tablespoon local, raw honey

1. In a juicer, juice the turmeric and ginger. If you're using a blender, you will need to use a nut bag to strain out the pulp. Discard the pulp into your compost bin or trash can.

2. With a hand juicer, juice the lemons and orange.

3. Combine all of the juice into a small bowl, add the piperine, MCT oil, and honey, and whisk together, until well combined.

4. Serve in 2 ounce mason jars or shot glasses. Can be stored in the fridge in an airtight container or mason jar for up to 5 days.

DETOX SHOT

MAKES: 2 shots // TOTAL TIME: 10 minutes

There are so many health benefits from the juice of both of these root veggies, including increasing your blood flow, reducing blood pressure, and detoxifying the body. If you don't have a juicer, you can use a blender and strain out the pulp to get your juice. Make sure to peel the veggies before juicing them to avoid the earthy taste.

1 small beet, peeled and quartered

1 large carrot, peeled

¼-inch piece of fresh ginger, peeled

1. In a juicer, juice the beet, carrot, and ginger. If you're using a blender, you will need to use a nut bag to strain out the pulp. Discard the pulp into your compost bin or trash can.

2. Serve in 2 ounce mason jars or shot glasses. Can be stored in the fridge in an airtight container or mason jar for up to 5 days.

GINGER-LEMONGRASS TEA

MAKES: 4 cups // TOTAL TIME: 25 minutes

This is one of my favorite bedtime drinks. Earlier this year, I made a pact with myself that I would drink something hot every night to help me wind down before bed. Now, it doesn't happen every night, but I do try to do it as much as I can. Anyone who knows me, knows I am a workaholic. If I have something that needs to get done, I will stay up until it's completed. Let's just say that during this cookbook-writing process, I have not been going to sleep at my normal bedtime. I stay up until about midnight or later every night working on photos and content, tweaking this or that, and creating fun new recipes. It can be served hot or iced, but my favorite is hot.

Tip: To smash lemongrass, cut off the tough bottom part and the top skinny part. Peel off the tough layers (you can cut a small slit down the stalk to help you peel it off). Once you're left with the inner part, lay it on a cutting board and smash it with a rolling pin or something similar; this will bring all of the juices out.

4 cups filtered water

2 stalks lemongrass, cut into 3-inch pieces and smashed

1-inch piece of ginger, peeled and sliced thin

Juice of ½ lemon

1 teaspoon local, raw honey

1. Bring the water to a boil in a small pot.

2. Place the ginger and lemongrass in the boiling water. Boil for 5 minutes, remove from heat, and add the lemon juice and honey. Let it steep, covered, for 10 minutes.

3. Strain out the ginger and lemongrass, and pour tea into a coffee mug. If serving cold, let cool to room temperature before serving over ice. Can be stored in the fridge in an airtight container or mason jar for up to 2 weeks.

MATCHA LATTE

MAKES: 2 cups // TOTAL TIME: 10 minutes

Matcha is becoming more and more popular. Now you can go and order a matcha latte at pretty much any coffee shop, but they're never as good as the ones I make at home. I love to make this as an afternoon pick-me-up or in the morning if I am feeling a little sluggish. It's full of flavor and gives you the boost you need to get through the day. I use the steamer on the espresso machine to steam the milk, but you can also heat the milk on the stove.

When you start looking for matcha online, there are so many choices. I use a big bag of cheaper matcha for my smoothies, but for my lattes, I choose a higher quality. A good matcha will cost you about $40–$50 for a two ounce can. You only need a tiny amount to make the latte, so the small containers that are expensive will actually last you a long time.

Tips: Using homemade nut milk will make this so much better.

1 ¾ cups almond milk (pg. 192), cashew milk (pg. 193) or nut milk of choice

¼ cup full-fat coconut milk, well shaken

1 Tablespoon vanilla syrup (Monin)

½ teaspoon matcha powder

Dollop of coconut whipped cream (pg. 241)

1. Pour all of the ingredients into a coffee mug and use your steamer to heat it up. It will take about 3 minutes.

2. If you do not have a steamer, heat all of the ingredients in a small pot over medium heat. Whisk frequently to make it frothy, about 5 minutes, or until hot. Be careful not to let it boil or it will become very thick. Pour into a coffee mug and add a dollop of coconut whipped cream for an extra flavor boost.

GOLDEN MILK

MAKES: 2 cups // TOTAL TIME: 10 minutes

I am usually go, go, go all day every day until I hit the pillow. One thing that I've been needing to do is slow down at night so I can get a good night's sleep. Drinking a golden milk helps me relax and get my mind off of everything I need to do. This drink is full of ingredients that are packed with amazing health benefits. Turmeric is a powerful anti-inflammatory and antioxidant and cinnamon can help relieve digestion discomfort. It's a great way to end your night.

Tips: Using homemade nut milk will make this so much better.

1 ½ cups almond milk (pg. 192), cashew milk (pg. 193) or nut milk of choice

½ cup full-fat coconut milk, well shaken

½ teaspoon ground turmeric

¼ teaspoon ground cinnamon

½ teaspoon vanilla powder

Tiny pinch of piperine (optional)

1 teaspoon maple syrup

Dollop of coconut whipped cream (pg. 241)

1. Pour all of the ingredients into a coffee mug and use your steamer to heat it up. It will take about 3 minutes.

2. If you do not have a steamer, heat all of the ingredients in a small pot over medium heat. Whisk frequently to make it frothy, about 5 minutes, or until hot. Be careful not to let it boil or it will become very thick. Pour into a coffee mug and add a dollop of coconut whipped cream for an extra flavor boost.

DESSERTS

CHOCOLATE CHIPLESS COOKIES

MAKES: 12 cookies // TOTAL TIME: 25 minutes

When I was growing up, I loved to bake with my mom. My favorite thing to bake was the recipe from the back of the Nestlé chocolate chip bag, but I would never add in any chocolate chips. Everything around the chocolate chips was my favorite part, so why add them in? Here you go: my childhood dream cookie turned gluten and dairy-free, for you to try. These are light, fluffy, and delicious.

1 cup turbinado sugar, plus more for sprinkling

½ cup Kerrygold or dairy-free butter, softened

1 large egg

1 Tablespoon cashew milk (pg. 193) or nut milk of choice

2 Tablespoons vanilla extract

¼ teaspoon sea salt

½ teaspoon xanthan gum

2 cups cassava flour

1. Preheat the oven to 350°F and line a baking sheet with reusable parchment paper.

2. In a stand mixer on medium speed, beat the sugar and butter until well combined.

3. Add in the egg, nut milk, vanilla, and salt. Turn the mixer to low and add the xanthan gum and flour; mix until well combined.

4. If you have time, cover the dough and put in the fridge for an hour. This makes the dough easier to work with. (If you don't have time, you can skip this step.)

5. Roll into 1 ½-inch balls and place on the baking sheet, leaving at least 1 inch between each ball. Sprinkle a little sugar on top.

6. Bake for 10-12 minutes or until a toothpick comes out clean. Remove from the oven and let the cookies cool.

7. Can be stored in the fridge in an airtight container for up to 5 days.

WATERMELON-LIME ICE POPS

MAKES: 8 ice pops // TOTAL TIME: 15 minutes

Everyone in our house loves these, especially the kids. They're great for a hot summer day. The best part is that they contain no added sugar, yet they hit the spot when you're craving something sweet.

Tip: Buy a silicone ice pop mold on Amazon. It makes the ice pops easy to store and they pop right out!

5 cups diced watermelon (from about half a medium-size watermelon)

Juice and grated zest of 2 limes

1. In a food processor or blender, blend all of the ingredients on high until smooth.

2. Pour the mixture into the silicone ice pop holders, and put the top on. Slide the sticks in with 2–3 inches sticking out.

3. Freeze overnight. Can be stored in the freezer for up to 1 month.

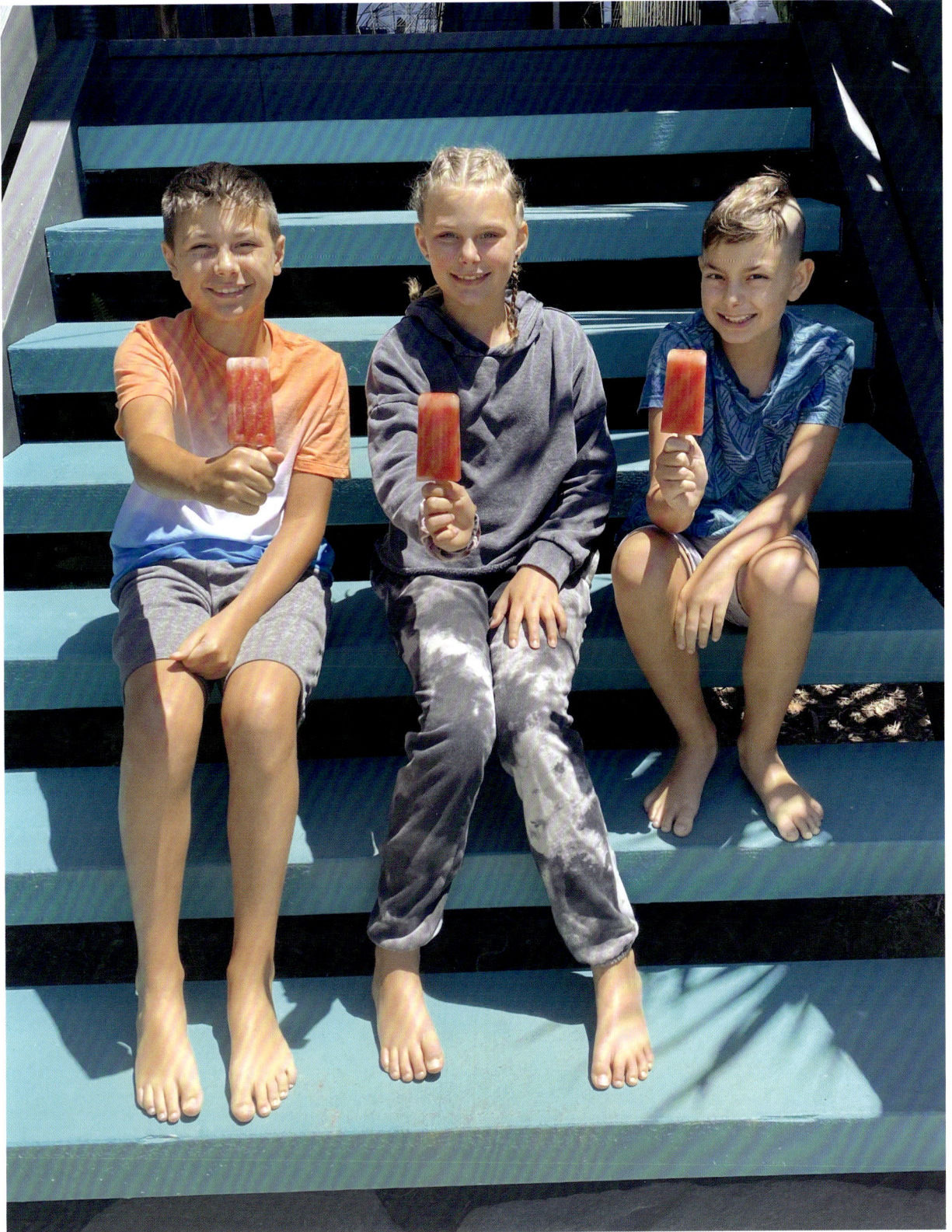

CASHEW BUTTER-CHOCOLATE CHIP COOKIES

MAKES: 12 cookies // TOTAL TIME: 20 minutes

These cookies are so easy, and everyone loves them. They have a gooey center, and the sea salt on top makes them the perfect mix of savory and sweet. I serve them at parties all the time, and no one knows they're gluten-free. People are always asking me for the recipe, so everyone, here you go! There are also really, really good without the chocolate chips.

Tips: You can use store-bought cashew butter, but I like to make my own. It's so simple to make and is actually much cheaper. You can also use almond butter, but cashew is the crowd favorite.

If saving for later, pop in the microwave for 20 seconds to heat up when ready to eat.

2 Tablespoons Kerrygold or dairy-free butter, softened

½ cup turbinado or coconut sugar

¼ cup cashew butter (pg. 196) or nut butter of choice

1 large egg

1 Tablespoon vanilla extract

¼ teaspoon sea salt

½ teaspoon baking soda

2 cups almond flour

½ cup vegan chocolate chips (Enjoy Life)

Flaky sea salt, for topping

1. Preheat the oven to 350°F and line a baking sheet with reusable parchment paper.

2. In a stand mixer on medium speed, beat the butter, sugar, nut butter, egg, and vanilla until well combined.

3. Add in the salt and baking soda. Turn the mixer to low and add in the almond flour. Mix until well combined.

4. Fold in the chocolate chips with a silicone spatula. Roll into 1 ½-inch balls (about 2 Tablespoons each), and arrange on the baking sheet, leaving about an inch between each cookie so they have room to spread. Lightly flatten each ball with your fingers and sprinkle sea salt on top.

5. Bake for 10–12 minutes. The cookies will still be slightly doughy in the middle. Let cool for a few minutes before eating. Can be stored in an airtight container for up to 5 days.

CHEESECAKE

MAKES: 9 servings // TOTAL TIME: 2 hours (plus 2 hours chilling)

I love cheesecake, and I was really bummed about not being able to eat it when I cut out dairy. Who would have thought there was such thing as a cheeseless cheesecake? And that it would taste just as good as the real thing! Don't be discouraged by the long cook time on this recipe; a lot of the time is just soaking or cooling.

Filling

1 cup raw cashews

1 cup coconut cream

8 oz dairy-free cream cheese (Kite Hill)

1 Tablespoon arrowroot powder

1 Tablespoon vanilla extract

⅔ cup maple syrup

1 Tablespoon coconut oil, melted

Grated zest of 1 lemon

2 Tablespoons freshly squeezed lemon juice

¼ teaspoon sea salt

Coconut whipped cream, for topping (pg. 241)

Crust

¾ cup gluten-free rolled oats

2 Tablespoons coconut sugar

¾ cup raw almonds

¼ teaspoon sea salt

4 Tablespoons coconut oil, melted, plus more as needed

1. To start the filling, place cashews in a bowl filled with boiling water and let sit for 1 hour.

2. In the meantime, make the crust: Preheat the oven to 350°F and line an 8x8-inch baking dish with reusable parchment paper.

3. Blend oats, coconut sugar, almonds, and salt in a food processor on high until well combined. Add the coconut oil, and blend until a dough is formed, scraping down the sides as necessary. If the dough is too dry, add 1 more Tablespoon coconut oil and blend again.

4. Transfer the dough to the baking dish and spread evenly on the bottom. To help flatten the crust, use reusable parchment paper and the flat bottom of a glass to make it smooth and even; press the dough up the sides to form a crust.

5. Bake the crust for 25 minutes, or until the edges are golden brown. Remove from the oven and let cool.

6. Reduce the oven heat to 325°F.

7. While the crust is baking, continue making the filling: Strain and rinse the cashews. Put them into a food processor or blender along with the rest of the filling ingredients. Blend on high until very creamy, about 2 minutes.

8. Once the crust has cooled, pour the filling over the crust and spread into an even layer. Give the pan a few taps on the counter to remove any air bubbles.

9. Bake for 1 hour, or until the edges look dry and the center is slightly jiggly. Take out of the oven and let sit for 15 minutes.

10. Put it in the fridge uncovered for 2 hours. Cover and let sit in the fridge overnight.

11. Slice and serve topped with coconut whipped cream. Can be stored in the fridge in an airtight container for up to 4 days.

COCONUT WHIPPED CREAM

MAKES: 3 cups // TOTAL TIME: 15 minutes (plus overnight chilling)

This whipped cream is so delicious and versatile. You can use it on any dessert, as a topping for a matcha latte, or just to eat by the spoonful if you want something sweet.

2 (13.5-oz) cans full-fat coconut milk, refrigerated overnight

1 Tablespoon maple syrup

1 Tablespoon vanilla extract

1. In a stand mixer with the whisk attachment, spoon the solid coconut cream from both cans into the bowl (save the remaining liquid in case you need to thin the whipped cream). Whisk on high speed for 2 minutes.

2. Use a silicone spatula to fold in the maple syrup and vanilla.

3. Serve immediately or store in the fridge in an airtight container for up to 2 weeks.

SARA'S LIME PIE

MAKES: one 8-inch pie // TOTAL TIME: 1 hour (plus overnight chilling)

We have 2 big lime trees at our house that produce tons of limes year-round. One of my good friends, Sara, came to visit me when we had a surplus of limes. She loves to bake, so we decided to put them to good use. That night, we baked this delicious lime pie. We ate it so quickly that we made another one before she left. I can't wait for you to try this one!

Filling

3 large eggs

½ cup maple syrup

½ cup full-fat coconut milk, well shaken

½ cup freshly squeezed lime juice

Grated zest of 1 lime, plus more for garnish

2 Tablespoons arrowroot powder

Coconut whipped cream, for topping (pg. 241)

Lime slices, for garnish

Crust

1 ½ cups almond flour

2 Tablespoons shredded unsweetened coconut

½ Tablespoon sea salt

2 Tablespoons maple syrup

2 Tablespoons coconut oil, melted

1. Preheat the oven to 350°F and line a pie pan with reusable parchment paper.

2. Make the crust: In a medium bowl, whisk together almond flour, coconut, and salt. In a separate large bowl, whisk together the maple syrup and coconut oil. A little at a time, add the dry ingredients to the wet ingredients, stirring with a silicone spatula until well combined.

3. Press the dough into bottom and up sides of the pie pan. Use a sheet of reusable parchment paper and the flat bottom of a glass to smooth it out and make it even. Bake for 12 minutes, or until golden brown. Let cool completely.

4. Reduce the oven heat to 325°F.

5. While the crust is baking, make the filling: In a large bowl, whisk together the eggs and maple syrup. Add the coconut milk, lime juice, lime zest, and arrowroot powder. Whisk until completely combined.

6. Once the crust has cooled, pour the filling into the crust. Give the pan a few taps on the counter to remove any air bubbles. Bake for 30–40 minutes, or until the pie is firm on the edges and a little jiggly in the center.

7. Refrigerate uncovered for at least 8 hours. Top with coconut whipped cream, some lime slices, and more lime zest. Can be stored in the fridge in an airtight container for up to 5 days.

Butter Cups

I should have these recipes under Staples, because that is what it is at our house. I make them almost every other day, and somehow we still run out. I swear I have some friends who invite themselves over just to get one! They're so easy, and they only need to stay in the freezer for about 25 minutes until they're ready to eat. The trick to all of these is to make the chocolate layers thin, so when you take them out of the freezer the chocolate layer is easy to break through with your teeth and there is a lot of creamy nut butter in the middle. You can make these with any nut butter you like, but my favorite is cashew butter. There are so many different combos to make these butter cups. You can add in the pretzels for an extra crunch, cayenne for extra spice, honey for extra sweetness. Try them all—you will not be disappointed!

Tip: Hop on over to Amazon and buy a silicone mini-muffin pan to use for all of the butter cup recipes; the butter cups pop out easily, and it's dishwasher safe.

CASHEW BUTTER CUPS

MAKES: 16 // TOTAL TIME: 15 minutes (plus 25 minutes freezing)

1 (10-oz) bag vegan chocolate chips (Enjoy Life)

1-2 Tablespoons cayenne powder (optional)

1 cup cashew butter (pg. 196) or nut butter of choice

16 gluten-free pretzel twists, plus more for topping (Glutino) (optional)

⅓ cup local, raw honey, plus more for topping

1 Tablespoon coconut oil, at room temperature

Coarse sea salt

1. In a glass bowl, heat up the chocolate for 30 seconds in the microwave; stir. Repeat 4–5 times until there are just a few chunks left; stir until they melt. Be careful not to overheat. If using cayenne powder, stir it into the melted chocolate.

2. Drizzle about a teaspoon of the melted chocolate into each cup of the silicone mini-muffin pan, just enough to cover the bottoms. Lightly tap the pan on the counter to spread it evenly.

3. Add 1 Tablespoon cashew butter to each cup; it should come almost to the top. Tap the pan again on the counter to make everything settle.

4. If using the pretzels, lay one on top of each butter cup, and drizzle a little honey on top. Add the coconut oil into the remaining chocolate, and stir until well combined (this will make the chocolate thinner and easy to drizzle).

5. Drizzle a little more chocolate on top to completely cover the pretzel (if using), honey, and cashew butter. Give the pan another tap on the counter to ensure there are no air bubbles and the chocolate is settled.

6. Add a drizzle of honey, a sprinkle of coarse sea salt, and a few pretzel pieces (if using) to the top of each cup. Chill in the freezer for 25 minutes before serving. Can be stored in the freezer in an airtight container for up to 1 month.

COCO BUTTER CUPS

MAKES: 16 // TOTAL TIME: 30 minutes (plus 25 minutes freezing)

1 (10-oz) bag vegan chocolate chips (Enjoy Life)

1 cup coconut butter, at room temperature

1 Tablespoon coconut oil, at room temperature

Coarse sea salt, for topping

Coconut shavings, for topping

1. In a glass bowl, heat up the chocolate for 30 seconds in the microwave; stir. Repeat 4–5 times until there are just a few chunks left; stir until they melt. Be careful not to overheat.

2. Drizzle about a teaspoon of the melted chocolate into each cup of the silicone mini-muffin pan, just enough to cover the bottoms. Lightly tap the pan on the counter to spread it evenly.

3. Add 1 Tablespoon coconut butter to each cup; it should come almost to the top. Tap the pan again on the counter to make everything settle.

4. Add the coconut oil to the remaining chocolate, and stir until well combined (this will make the chocolate thinner and easy to drizzle). Drizzle a little more chocolate on top of the coconut butter to cover it completely. Tap the pan once more on the counter to get rid of any air bubbles and settle the chocolate.

5. Add a little sprinkle of coarse sea salt and coconut shavings to the top of each cup.

6. Chill in the freezer for at least 25 minutes before serving. Can be stored in the freezer in an airtight container for up to 1 month.

NBJ CUPS

MAKES: 16 // TOTAL TIME: 30 minutes (plus 25 minutes freezing)

1 (10-oz) bag vegan chocolate chips (Enjoy Life)

½ cup nut butter of choice

½ cup jelly of choice

1 Tablespoon coconut oil, at room temperature

Local, raw honey, for drizzling

Coarse sea salt, for topping

1. In a glass bowl, heat up the chocolate in the microwave for 30 seconds; stir. Repeat 4–5 times until there are just a few chunks left; stir until they melt. Be careful not to overheat.

2. Drizzle about a teaspoon of the melted chocolate into each cup of the silicone mini-muffin pan, just enough to cover the bottom. Lightly tap the pan on the counter to spread it evenly.

3. Add ½ Tablespoon nut butter and ½ Tablespoon jelly to each cup; it should come almost to the top.

4. Add the coconut oil to the remaining chocolate, and stir until well combined (this will make the chocolate thinner and easy to drizzle). Drizzle a little more chocolate on top of the nut butter and jelly to cover them completely. Give the pan one more tap to release any air bubbles and settle the chocolate.

5. Add a little sprinkle of coarse sea salt to the top of each cup. Drizzle some honey over the top.

6. Chill in the freezer for at least 25 minutes before serving. Can be stored in the freezer in an airtight container for up to 1 month.

CHOCOLATE AVOCADO PROTEIN PUDDING

MAKES: 2-3 cups // TOTAL TIME: 35 minutes

About 10 years ago, I found a chocolate canned protein pudding at GNC that I loved. I ate so much of it that I got burned out on it and totally forgot about it. When I moved out to California, I read about chocolate avocado pudding and had to give it a try. By adding in protein, you're getting an extra protein boost while enjoying dessert. It's delicious, and the kids have no idea they're eating a healthy dessert.

2 large, ripe avocados, peeled, pitted and sliced

2 scoops unflavored collagen protein powder (Bulletproof)

½ cup unsweetened cacao powder

¼ cup coconut sugar

⅓ cup full-fat coconut milk, well shaken

2 teaspoons vanilla extract

⅛ teaspoon ground cinnamon

1. Put all of the ingredients into a blender or food processor and blend on high until smooth, about 1 minute.

2. Refrigerate pudding until chilled. Can be stored in the fridge in an airtight container for up to 3 days.

CHOCOLATE FRUIT CLUSTERS

MAKES: 12 // TOTAL TIME: 35 minutes

You can put so many twists on this simple recipe, and no matter what fruit you use, it's going to be delicious. Every time I make these for a get-together, people always ask for more and for the recipe on their way out. I try to always have a batch in the freezer, because they're such a good, healthy snack to have on hand to satisfy a sweet tooth.

½ (10-oz) bag vegan chocolate chips or chunks (Enjoy Life)

1 Tablespoon coconut oil, at room temperature

2 cups berries of choice (blueberries and raspberries are my favorite)

Coarse sea salt, for garnish

Local, raw honey, for garnish (optional)

1. Line a baking sheet with reusable parchment paper. In a glass bowl, heat the chocolate for 30 seconds; stir. Repeat 4–5 times until there are only a few chunks left; stir until they melt. Be careful not to overheat.

2. Add the coconut oil to the remaining chocolate, and stir until well combined (this will make the chocolate thinner and easy to drizzle). Spoon small dollops of chocolate on the parchment paper, making circles about 1 ½ inches apart from one another.

3. Top each chocolate dollop with 5–7 berries and drizzle chocolate over the top. Sprinkle with sea salt and drizzle with honey, if using.

4. Chill in the freezer for about 25 minutes before serving. Can be stored in the freezer in an airtight container or up to 2 weeks.

CHOCOLATE-CASHEW BUTTER PIE

MAKES: one 8-inch pie // TOTAL TIME: 45 minutes

This no-bake dessert tastes just like cashew butter cookie dough. It's gooey and oh so delicious. It can be made with peanut, cashew, or almond butter; but my go-to is cashew butter.

Cashew Butter Layer

¾ cup cashew butter (pg. 196) or nut butter of choice

¼ cup coconut oil, at room temperature

¼ cup maple syrup

1 Tablespoon vanilla extract

½ teaspoon sea salt

2 ½ cups almond flour

1 Tablespoon maca powder

½ cup vegan chocolate chips (Enjoy Life)

Chocolate Layer

1 ½ cups raw walnuts

2 Tablespoons unsweetened cacao powder

½ teaspoon sea salt

9 Medjool dates, pitted

Flaky sea salt, for topping

1. Line an 8-inch pie pan with reusable parchment paper.

2. Make the nut butter layer: In a large bowl, mix together the nut butter, coconut oil, maple syrup, vanilla, and salt until well combined. Add the almond flour and maca powder and stir to combine. You can use your hands when it gets thick and hard to stir. Fold in the chocolate chips with a silicone spatula.

3. Place the nut butter mixture into the pan and use a sheet of reusable parchment paper and the flat bottom of a glass to make it smooth and even. Place in the freezer.

4. Make the chocolate layer: In a food processor or blender, add the walnuts, cacao powder, salt, and dates. Blend on high until well combined, scraping down the sides as necessary. If the mixture is too thick and getting stuck, add 1 Tablespoon water and blend again.

5. Spread the chocolate mixture over the nut butter layer and use reusable parchment paper and the flat bottom of a glass to make it smooth and even. Freeze for another 30 minutes, then cut into pie slices. Can be stored in the fridge or freezer in an airtight container for up to 1 week.

BLACK BEAN BROWNIES

MAKES: 8-10 brownies // TOTAL TIME: 25 minutes

No one would ever guess that these seemingly decadent brownies are made with black beans. Not only do you get your chocolate craving satisfied, but you also get all the fiber, protein, and antioxidants from the beans. They have a gooey center and are best served warm.

1 (15-oz) can black beans, drained and rinsed

2 Tablespoons cacao powder

½ cup gluten-free rolled oats

¼ teaspoon Himalayan salt

⅓ cup maple syrup

2 Tablespoons coconut sugar

1 Tablespoon vanilla extract

½ teaspoon baking powder

½ cup vegan chocolate chips, plus more for topping (Enjoy Life)

1. Preheat the oven to 350°F and line an 8-inch pie pan with reusable parchment paper.

2. Combine all ingredients (except the chocolate chips) into a food processor or blender. Blend on high until completely smooth, around 1–2 minutes. Fold in the chocolate chips with a silicone spatula.

3. Pour the mixture into the pie pan and give the pan a couple taps on the counter to release any air bubbles.

4. Bake for 15–18 minutes, or until a toothpick poked in the center comes out clean. Let cool before topping with chocolate chips. Can be stored in the fridge in an airtight container for up to 5 days.

CHOCOLATE PRETZEL BARK

MAKES: about 1 pound bark // TOTAL TIME: 25 minutes

How hard is it for you to resist all of those yummy treats on display in the checkout line at the store? I used to always throw a bag of chocolate bark in my cart while I was waiting. I would end up finishing the bag on my three minute drive home, and I'd feel terrible afterwards because they're full of crap, including dairy and gluten. So I decided to start making my own. It's so damn simple; I can't believe I hadn't tried it before. You can throw just about anything in the chocolate, but this is my favorite combo.

1 (10-oz) bag vegan chocolate chips (Enjoy Life)

1 Tablespoon coconut oil, at room temperature

1 cup gluten-free pretzels (Glutino)

¼ cup dried blueberries, or berry of choice

½ cup raw pecans or raw nut of choice

2 Tablespoons coconut shavings

1 Tablespoon flaky sea salt

2 Tablespoons local, raw honey

1. Line a rimmed baking sheet with reusable parchment paper.

2. In a glass bowl, heat the chocolate in the microwave for 30 seconds; stir. Repeat 4–5 times, or until there are only a few chunks left; stir to melt the rest. Be careful not to overheat. Add in the coconut oil and stir to combine.

3. Pour ¾ of the melted chocolate onto the parchment paper and smooth with a spoon or silicone spatula.

4. Place the pretzels and pecans in a quart-size plastic bag. Use a rolling pin or something similar to crush into small chunks. Sprinkle the chunks and the dried blueberries on top of the chocolate layer. Drizzle the remaining chocolate over the top and sprinkle with coconut shavings and sea salt. Drizzle honey to top it off.

5. Chill in the freezer for 30 minutes. Can be stored in the freezer in an airtight container for up to 2 weeks.

GRAB & GO SNACKS

PROTEIN BARS

MAKES: 8 bars // TOTAL TIME: 10 minutes (plus 1 hour freezing)

With both my husband and me being so busy, sometimes I don't have time to come home and make lunch, or lunch doesn't get started until about 3 p.m. Having healthy snacks like these protein bars at the house helps us power through those times when we are in need of something quick and healthy.

Crust

2 cups raw, unsalted cashews

1 cup cashew butter (pg. 196) or nut butter of choice

2 scoops unflavored protein powder (Bulletproof)

2 Tablespoons shaved coconut

1 Tablespoon maple syrup

1 teaspoon vanilla powder

1 teaspoon ground cinnamon

Topping

1 cup raw almonds

6 Medjool dates, pitted

1 cup dried blueberries

¼ cup raw pumpkin seeds

¼ cup dried goji berries

2 Tablespoons shaved coconut

2 scoops unflavored protein powder (Bulletproof)

2 Tablespoons maple syrup

1. Line a 7x9-inch rimmed baking sheet with reusable parchment paper.

2. Combine all of the ingredients for the crust in a food processor or blender, and pulse until well combined, scraping down the edges as necessary. Press the dough into the baking sheet to create a ½-inch-thick layer. Use a sheet of reusable parchment paper and the flat bottom of a glass to make it even and smooth.

3. Add all of the topping ingredients into the same food processor or blender and pulse for about 2 minutes, or until well combined and sticky.

4. Spread the topping mixture over the cashew crust, pressing gently until smooth and even.

5. Chill in the freezer for 1 hour. Cut into bars. Can be stored in the fridge or freezer in an airtight container for up to 2 weeks.

Protein Balls

These are great snacks to have in the fridge for a grab-and-go when you're hungry and in a hurry or if you have kids who are always scouring the fridge for something to snack on. There are tons of delicious recipes for protein balls, but here I've included some of my favorites.

COCONUT CACAO BALLS

MAKES: 10 balls // TOTAL TIME: 10 minutes (plus 20 minutes freezing)

10 Medjool dates, pitted

½ cup shredded coconut, plus more for topping

2 Tablespoons cacao powder

¼ cup hemp seeds

2 Tablespoons nut milk of choice (pg. 192) or water

2 scoops unflavored collagen protein powder (Bulletproof)

Combine all ingredients in a food processor and blend on high until well combined and starts to form into one giant ball, scraping down the sides as necessary. Form into 1-inch balls then roll in more coconut, if you wish. Chill in the freezer for 20 minutes. Can be stored in the fridge in an airtight container for up to 1 week or in the freezer for up to 1 month.

MATCHA ENERGY BALLS

MAKES: 10 balls // TOTAL TIME: 10 minutes (plus 20 minutes freezing)

8 Medjool dates, pitted

1 Tablespoon matcha powder

½ cup shredded coconut, plus more for topping

¼ cup almond flour

¼ cup hemp seeds

2 scoops unflavored collagen protein powder (Bulletproof)

1 Tablespoon vanilla extract

2 Tablespoons nut milk of choice (pg. 192) or filtered water

Combine all ingredients in a food processor and blend on high until well combined and starts to form into one giant ball, scraping down the sides as necessary. Form into 1-inch balls then roll in more coconut, if you wish. Chill in the freezer for 20 minutes. Can be stored in the fridge in an airtight container for up to 1 week or in the freezer for up to 1 month.

BLUEBERRY-VANILLA PROTEIN BALLS

MAKES: 10 balls // TOTAL TIME: 10 minutes (plus 20 minutes freezing)

1 cup cashew butter (pg. 196) or nut butter of choice

1 Tablespoon vanilla extract

2 scoops unflavored collagen protein powder (Bulletproof)

2 Medjool dates, pitted

½ cup dried blueberries

1 teaspoon flaky sea salt

Combine the nut butter, vanilla, protein powder, and dates in a food processor and blend on high until well combined and starts to form into one giant ball, scraping down the sides as necessary. Fold in the blueberries and salt with a silicone spatula. Roll into 1-inch balls and top with a sprinkle of flaky sea salt. Chill in the freezer for 20 minutes. Can be stored in the fridge in an airtight container for up to 1 week or in the freezer for up to 1 month.

CASHEW BUTTER BALLS

MAKES: 10 balls // TOTAL TIME: 10 minutes (plus 20 minutes freezing)

1 cup cashew butter (pg. 196) or nut butter of choice

¼ cup coconut flour

¼ cup raw cashews

¼ cup raw almonds

¼ cup maple syrup

1 Tablespoon vanilla extract

1 teaspoon sea salt, plus more for topping

½ cup vegan chocolate chips (Enjoy Life)

Add all of the ingredients (except the chocolate chips) into a food processor. Blend on high until well combined and starts to form into one giant ball, scraping down the sides as necessary. Fold in the chocolate chips with a silicone spatula. Roll the dough into 1-inch balls. Sprinkle each ball with sea salt and chill in the freezer for 20 minutes. Can be stored in the fridge in an airtight container for up to 1 week or in the freezer for up to 1 month.

FOUR-LEGGED FRIENDS

ROBINSON RANCH DOG FOOD

MAKES: 14 meals for 60lb dog // TOTAL TIME: 45 minutes

This has become such a hit at our house; our dogs go crazy for this food. My German shepherd, Ruqa, used to have really bad skin allergies. We had tried everything—steroids, shots, every kind of food you can imagine—and nothing was working. I began the journey to find a good homemade dog food recipe that has all the protein and nutrients that she needed to stay healthy. After lots of trial and error, I finally found a combo that worked. I am not saying this is the perfect mix for every dog, but after eating this food for about four months, she got off all of her meds and shots and she has never looked better. I double the recipe and make two weeks at a time, storing the second week in the freezer. If you save your eggshells, you can bake them and powder them in a food processor and add into your dog food for added calcium.

Tips: Your food processor has a shred disk attachment that sits at the top of the processor bowl. Use this to shred all of the zucchini and carrots for the dog food. Also, use a rice cooker for the rice. Both are huge time-savers.

You can find the B6 tablets and salmon oil on Amazon.

2 ½ cups brown rice

1 ½ Tablespoons ground eggshells, from about 2–3 eggs (optional)

5 B6 50 mg tablets (optional)

5 lb ground turkey or chicken

2 (16-oz) bags fresh or frozen peas

1 (16-oz) bag fresh spinach

3 large zucchinis, shredded

5 large carrots, shredded

1 (16-oz) bag frozen French-style or fresh (chopped) green beans

3-4 Tablespoons Wild Alaskan salmon oil (Vital Pet for Life)

14 reusable 16-oz plastic containers

1. Cook the rice according to the package instructions.

2. To bake the eggshells, preheat the oven to 175°F and line a baking sheet with reusable parchment paper. Spread the eggshells on the baking sheet and bake for 10 minutes; the shells will become brittle. Let them cool, then place in the food processor or blender and blend on high until powdered. I do this in bulk and store them in a Mason jar for easy future use.

3. Wash the food processor or blender and place the B6 pills in. Blend on high until powdered. Make sure to use tablets, not capsules, and remove the silica packet; you don't want any plastic in there. I also do this in bulk, and store in a pepper shaker for easy future use.

4. Place ground turkey in a large stockpot over medium-high heat. Cover and let cook for about 15 minutes, or until cooked through, stirring occasionally and breaking it apart.

5. In a large tub, mix together the peas, spinach, zucchinis, carrots, and green beans. If you don't have a large tub, you can use a few large foil roasting pans; they're big and easy to clean.

6. Strain the grease from the turkey and pour the meat on top of the veggies; add the rice as well. Stir it all together until well combined, you may need to use your hands. Fill up each 16-oz reusable container with food, ¼ teaspoon ground eggshell, ¹⁄₁₆ teaspoon B6 powder, and ½ teaspoon Wild Alaskan salmon oil (if using the pump container 1 pump per meal) on top of each container; secure with the tops.

7. Store in the fridge and serve one at breakfast and one at dinner. If making two weeks at a time, store the second week in the freezer in an airtight container.

Disclaimer: I am not a dog expert, and this may not work for all dogs. I feed this to mine because I would rather give them real food rather than kibble. Talk to your vet if you have any questions or concerns.

DOG TREATS

MAKES: 25 // TOTAL TIME: 25 minutes

My dogs love these. They know when I am making them and stand right at my feet for any dropped dough. When they're done, I store them in the fridge, so anytime I open the fridge, the dogs are there waiting, thinking it's treat time. These are packed with healthy fats to give your dog's coat that extra shine. They're super easy to make and so much better for your dog than the store-bought treats. You can also double the recipe and freeze the second batch for later use.

1 ½ cups coconut flour, plus more for rolling

½ cup organic peanut butter

3 eggs

½ cup coconut oil, at room temperature

1 cup canned pumpkin

1. Preheat the oven to 350°F and line a baking sheet with reusable parchment paper.

2. Combine all ingredients in a stand mixer and mix on high until well combined, about 2 minutes.

3. Dust a cutting board and rolling pin lightly with coconut flour. Place the dough on the board and roll out to a ¼- to ½-inch thickness, using more flour as needed to make the dough not stick.

4. Use your favorite cookie cutter to cut out the treats. Make sure to dip your cookie cutter in coconut flour often to avoid the dough sticking to the cutter.

5. Arrange cookies on the baking sheet and bake for 12 minutes, or until the edges become golden brown. Let cool, then store in an airtight container in the fridge for up to 2 weeks.

FOUR-LEGGED BIRTHDAY CAKE

MAKES: 1 dog cake // TOTAL TIME: 40 minutes

Who doesn't love to throw their dog a party? I love my animals so much that they get a party every year. This cake is such a treat for the pups, but it's also packed with healthy ingredients. You can make it in any baking pan, but I love to use a silicone dog bone pan to add to the theme. You can buy them on Amazon.

Cake

Avocado oil cooking spray

1 cup coconut flour

½ teaspoon baking soda

2 Tablespoons coconut oil, melted

¼ cup organic peanut butter

½ cup applesauce

½ cup canned pumpkin

1 egg

Raw pumpkin seeds, for topping

Coconut shavings, for topping

Frosting

¼ cup arrowroot powder

¼ cup filtered water

1 Tablespoon local, raw honey

2 Tablespoons organic peanut butter

1. Preheat the oven to 350°F and grease a silicone dog bone or 8-inch cake pan with cooking spray.

2. Make the cake: In a small bowl, whisk together the coconut flour and baking soda. In a large bowl, whisk together coconut oil, peanut butter, applesauce, pumpkin, and egg until well combined.

3. Slowly add the dry ingredients into the wet ingredients, stirring until well combined.

4. Pour the mixture into the dog bone and smooth with a spoon or silicone spatula. Bake for 25 minutes, or until a toothpick poked in the center comes out clean. Turn out onto a rack to cool completely.

5. Meanwhile, in a medium bowl, combine all of the frosting ingredients and whisk until well combined. It will thicken after sitting for about 8 minutes.

6. Once cooled, spread with the frosting, and add the toppings. Can be stored in the fridge in an airtight container for up to 5 days.

BEAUTY

HYDRATING BODY LOTION

MAKES: about 16 ounces // TOTAL TIME: 30 minutes

All my life, I've had dry skin. I searched high and low for a good lotion and could never find one that worked. Now that I've started making lotion, I don't know what I would do without it. This hydrating lotion is made with all-natural ingredients and is the answer to my dry skin. It's quick and easy to whip up. You can double or even triple this recipe and have a few backup jars.

I use lavender for fragrance, but you can use any essential oil you like, or you can cut the essential oil and go with an unscented lotion. I also like peppermint and lemongrass.

1 cup unrefined, pure shea butter, at room temperature

1 cup organic, unrefined coconut oil, at room temperature

1 Tablespoon vitamin E oil

1 Tablespoon almond oil

75–100 drops lavender essential oil, or oil of choice

1 (16-oz) Mason jar

1. Bring a pot of water to a boil over high heat. Place the shea butter in a glass bowl that will fit over the top of the pot. Set the bowl over the water, and steam to soften the shea butter, stirring until fully melted.

2. Place the coconut oil, vitamin E oil, almond oil, and lavender in a stand mixer with a whisk attachment. Transfer the melted shea butter to the mixer, and whisk on low until the coconut oil is completely melted and everything is well combined.

3. Pour into a Mason jar, close the lid, and chill in the fridge for 1 hour. You want it to be a soft solid. Remove from the fridge. You can use it immediately, but the texture is at its best 24–48 hours after. Store in an airtight container at room temperature for up to 6 months.

Bath Soaks, Scrubs & Salts

Wanting to take a trip to the spa but don't have the time or the means? Make a great bath soak, scrub, or salt at home and turn your own bathroom into a relaxing spa. These simple recipes can be made with all-natural ingredients that you more than likely already have in your kitchen. They're easy to mix up and make for great gifts. Every recipe in this beauty section is safe to use on your skin, contains no preservatives, and contains only a few natural ingredients.

Tip: When buying coconut oil, look for organic, unrefined coconut oil, which is less processed and thus retains its beneficial properties. When buying shea butter, look for unrefined pure shea butter. It should be ivory or yellowish in color.

Disclaimer: When using scrubs and anything with coconut oil in the bathtub please be careful, as it will leave the surface slippery.

RELAXING BATH SOAK

Light a few candles, turn on some relaxing spa music, and bask in all the goodness. This soak will have you lying in pure bliss. The Dead Sea salt will help the body get rid of toxins that have been trapped below the skin's surface. Himalayan salt stimulates cell growth, assists with detoxification, and improves circulation. The essential oils and dried flowers bring aromatherapy and relaxation. You can create endless combinations of essential oils and dried herbs/flowers to this basic scrub; you can also sub Epsom salts for Dead Sea salt.

Tip: If using any dried flowers or herbs, secure your serving of soak in a tea bag or a cheesecloth to avoid having a mess to clean up after your relaxing bath.

1 cup Dead Sea salt

½ cup Himalayan sea salt

20–40 drops essential oil of choice

1 Tablespoon dried flowers (optional)

1 Tablespoon dried herbs (optional)

Zest of citrus fruit of choice (optional)

Place all the ingredients into a large bowl. Toss with clean hands or a rubber spatula. Store in a mason jar or an airtight container for up to 6 months. Create a fun paper label if desired.

Use Instructions: Add 1 cup of soak into a warm bath. Lie back, relax, and enjoy.

Bath soak favorite combos:

Relaxing – peppermint & eucalyptus oils with dried eucalyptus leaves

Energizing – lemon & orange oils with dried rosemary and orange zest

Loving – rose oil with dried rose petals

Balancing – lemon & lavender oils with dried lavender and lemon zest

COCONUT MILK SOAK

This coconut milk soak will have your skin feeling silky smooth. Oatmeal acts as a protective barrier for your skin. It binds to it and helps hold in moisture and works as an anti-inflammatory. All these ingredients work together to ease irritated skin, balance pH, and leave your skin feeling super soft and moisturized. This is a great soak for babies and adults.

Tip: Secure your serving of coconut milk soak in a tea bag or a cheesecloth to avoid having a mess to clean up after your relaxing bath.

1 cup powdered coconut milk

¼ cup baking soda

½ cup oatmeal

20 drops essential oil of choice (optional)

A few oils to choose from:

Lavender – relieves stress

Chamomile – boosts mood

Sandalwood – reduces muscle aches and inflammation

Peppermint – cools, reduces skin irritations

Eucalyptus – relaxes

Place all the ingredients into a large bowl. Toss with clean hands or a rubber spatula. Store in a mason jar or an airtight container for up to 6 months. Create a fun paper label if desired.

Use Instructions: Add 1 cup of soak to a warm bath. Relax and enjoy the benefits.

Body Scrubs

Body scrubs are great to have on hand in the shower or the bath. They're amazing at removing dead skin cells, which allows you to absorb moisturizer better. They help the skin look brighter and tighter, giving you that radiant glow. They can unclog pores and prevent ingrown hairs. There are so many great benefits to using these scrubs on your skin. I recommend exfoliating with a body scrub two to three times per week.

MINTY-LIME SUGAR SCRUB

Is your skin looking a little dull? Use this scrub all over your body to help bring it back to life. You hear all the time that white sugar is bad for you, but when you use it on your skin instead of ingesting it, it has a lot of benefits. The small particles make for a great exfoliant to help get rid of dead skin, and the coconut oil will lock in the moisture. Mint is great for cooling and reducing inflammation, while the limes contain vitamin C and flavonoids, which are antioxidants that strengthen collagen.

1 cup granulated white sugar

¼ cup organic, unrefined coconut oil, at room temperature

1 Tablespoon chopped mint

1 Tablespoon fresh squeezed lime juice

Grated zest of 1 lime

10 drops peppermint essential oil

Combine all the ingredients in a large bowl and mix with a hand mixer or a fork. Store in a mason jar or an airtight container for up to 3 months. Create a fun paper label if desired.

Use Instructions: Thoroughly clean the skin with soap and water. Take a generous scoop, and gently scrub in a circular motion on any part of your body you wish to exfoliate. Rinse with clean water. Apply moisturizer afterwards.

BROWN SUGAR COOKIE SCRUB

This is my all-time favorite scrub. It smells so damn good. I love using turbinado sugar because it's more coarse and helps remove dead skin cells, leaving me with bright, glowing skin. You can also use regular white granulated sugar or brown sugar, which is finer and has antibacterial properties that help your skin stay clear and hydrated.

1 cup turbinado, brown or sugar of choice

½ cup Himalayan sea salt

3 Tablespoons almond oil

2 Tablespoons organic, unrefined coconut oil, at room temperature

1 Tablespoon vanilla extract

Combine all ingredients in a bowl and mix with a hand mixer or a fork. Store in a mason jar or an airtight container for up to 3 months. Create a fun paper label if desired.

Use Instructions: Thoroughly clean the skin with soap and water. Take a generous scoop, and gently scrub in a circular motion on any part of your body you wish to exfoliate. Rinse with clean water. Apply moisturizer afterwards.

LIP SCRUB

Homemade lip scrubs exfoliate your lips, removing dry and dead skin and leaving them moisturized and nourished. Your lips will be looking fuller, healthier, and more hydrated. This easy lip scrub can be mixed together in 5 minutes using only a few all-natural ingredients that you're going to want to lick right off when you're done.

1 Tablespoon organic, unrefined coconut oil, at room temperature

2 Tablespoons white sugar

1 teaspoon local, raw honey

Combine all ingredients in a bowl and mix together with a fork. Store in a mason jar or an airtight container for up to 3 months. Create a fun paper label if desired.

Use Instructions: Using one finger, scoop up a generous amount of lip scrub and gently rub in circular motion for about 30 seconds. Wash off the remainder of the scrub and finish off by applying some coconut oil or lip balm.

My Preferred Substitutions

Sour cream – Tofutti

Mozzarella – Miyoko's

Cream cheese –Kite Hill

Flour – coconut, cassava, or almond flour

Milk – cashew, almond or walnut

English muffins – Glutino (sooo good!)

Butter – Earth Balance

Corn chips – taro chips

Cheesy flavor – nutritional yeast

Noodles – Taste Republic gluten-free noodles

Chocolate chips - Enjoy Life

Yogurt - So Delicious

Pretzels - Glutino

Tips & Tricks

- Reusable parchment paper is better for the environment than disposable. You can also cut down to fit your baking sheets and pans and reuse over and over.

- Grind your own chicken. I love to buy chicken breasts and grind them in the food processor. I know I am getting quality meat, and it only takes a couple of minutes.

- Cook with avocado oil cooking spray. It has a high burn point.

- Buy air-chilled chicken. It produces tastier, more tender chicken, and the breasts aren't bulked up with excess water (which would cause them to become dry when cooked).

- Try to avoid the microwave but if you need to heat something up, use a glass bowl. I've gotten rid of all of my plastic Tupperware and replaced it with glass.

- Buy wild-caught fish. It's so much better for you than farm-raised, as they're less prone to disease or illness and are usually leaner and higher in fatty acids.

- Spray the baking sheet with cooking spray before lining with reusable parchment paper, and the parchment will stick and not roll up.

- Have all of your shake ingredients in easy, scoopable containers right by your NutriBullet.

- To julienne basil, stack the leaves, roll them like a cigar, and slice. This helps keep the oils intact and saves the flavor.

- Save your eggshells. Bake at 175°F for 10 minutes and grind in the food processor until powdered. You can add to your dog food for extra calcium, add to your chicken feed for better egg production, or spread in the garden to get rid of pests.

- Blend pretzels or gluten-free panko in the NutriBullet or food processor until powdered. This adds a good flavor and makes it easier to coat whatever you're wanting to "fry" in the oven or air fryer.

- Keep a jug of fruit-infused water on the counter daily to remind you to drink it.

- Combine your turmeric with piperine and sea salt to help your body get the anti-inflammatory benefits of the turmeric.

- Invest in a rice cooker; it makes perfect rice every time, and it's so easy.

- Spray the inside of a measuring cup with cooking spray before measuring something sticky; it will pour right out.

- To help crisp up romaine lettuce, chop off the bottom of the stem end, place the head in a measuring cup, and add enough cold water so just the cut end is submerged. Let sit for 30 minutes.

- To store strawberries, put them—unwashed and untrimmed—in a Mason jar or airtight container in the fridge. They'll stay fresh for up to 2 ½ weeks.

- Shred potatoes/veggies in a food processor with the shred disk attachment that sits on top of the processor bowl. Such a time saver.

- Shred chicken breasts easily in a food processor or with a hand mixer.

Composting

Creating something useful out of what you normally put in the trash is pretty cool. Instead of throwing away all of your food scraps and waste from your yard, make something that can be useful to your garden, trees, and house plants.

Composting is fun and relatively easy, once you get the hang of it. When I first tried it, I purchased a tumbler and didn't do much research. I would throw my food in the tumbler every few days, or whenever I would think of it, and never remember to turn it. I had no idea that you needed to add more than just food scraps to make compost.

After about two months, brown stuff was oozing out of the tumbler, and it smelled like death. What I had created was so foul that we had to hire someone to come over and throw it away. I threw in the towel for about a year, until I got the urge to give it another try. Here is a little guide to help you get started on composting.

For starters, I have a bowl that sits behind my sink to remind me to throw all of my scraps in it. With a family of five, we have a lot of scraps. Pretty much all scraps, except meat or bones, goes into the container. I dump my food scraps into my green bin (see below) nightly.

For my garden/yard waste, I separate the greens and browns into two trash cans. Browns are anything like leaves, sticks, woody material, straw, hay, cardboard, paper, and even dryer lint. Greens are grass clippings, plant clippings, coffee grounds, food scraps, weeds, eggshells, and animal poop (as long as the animal does not eat meat). Make sure to break anything large down into four to six inch pieces with a machete or clippers so it can decompose easily. One time-saving tip is to clip everything before you throw it into the trash can, so you are not stuck clipping everything right when you want to start your pile. This way you can fill the cans up as the weeks go on, and they're organized and ready to go when you're ready to start building your compost pile.

If possible, when choosing where you want to put your pile, make sure you're putting it in an area that is out of sight or around a corner. Compost piles are not the prettiest, but man are they useful. You also want to make sure you have space right next to the pile so you can turn the pile easily if needed. When doing thermophilic, or "hot," composting, where you are encouraging the decomposition of organic material with heat-loving bacteria, starting a pile during the warm months of the year is best. This way it can heat up easily and decompose faster. If it's really cold, you will want to save up your materials and start a pile in spring or summer, so the bacteria doesn't go dormant; the hard-working bacteria can go dormant if it's too hot as well.

You start by just placing one layer of woody material straight onto the ground. Woody material can be anything such as old branches, woody plants that have died, tree limbs, or twigs. You then layer brown, green, brown, and green, watering in-between. Make sure you have a little more than 50% browns in the pile compared to greens in order to achieve the right balance.

I've found that adding fresh grass clippings to the pile makes it heat up and break down fast! They're a high-nitrogen source as well as a great source of slow-release moisture. When you add grass clippings, you want to make sure you're spreading them out nicely and not just throwing them in clumps. When the balance is right, you can get compost without ever having to flip the pile.

When you are layering the pile, use a hose and spray in between each layer. Just a good eight to ten second spray on the shower setting will be good. Once you have all of your materials in the pile, use a pitchfork to bring the material from the edges to the top, making the pile as tall as possible. You want it to look like a teepee. Once you have it as tall as it will go (try to get it at least three feet tall), water one more time. Spray it on the shower setting for about ten seconds and then cover the pile with a tarp, a large burlap square, or anything that you have lying around the house that will cover it up to keep the heat in and the rain out. You do not want your pile too wet. Some say a good level of moisture for compost is that of lightly wrung-out sponge. If you squeeze hard, some moisture will come out, but it shouldn't be dripping water on its own unless you are just building it.

How often you turn your pile really depends on what is in it and how fast it's decomposing. I would recommend ordering a compost thermometer on Amazon and sticking the thermometer in the middle of the pile so you can see how active and hot it is. Once the pile starts to cool down (90°F or below), you should turn it to activate it to heat up again. A successful compost pile needs enough, but not too much, water and air to decompose. If you do not have a compost thermometer, then I would recommend turning your pile once a week.

Turning your pile is pretty simple and a good workout. All you need is a pitchfork and a little muscle. Little by little, you take the top off with the pitchfork and place it in the empty spot next to the pile. You do this until you have turned the whole pile upside down, so that now the bottom is on the top and the top on the bottom. Once you're done, give it a good shower with the hose, stick the thermometer in, and cover it back up.

You know that your pile is working when it's hot and the size of the pile starts shrinking. You will know your compost is ready when it's dark brown and crumbly and smells like rich, dark earth rather than being stinky. Storing your compost is easy, just leave it on the ground covered up by a tarp to prevent excess moisture from rain and snow runoff, but allow a little bit of humidity to get in and keep the pile damp. You want to use the compost within three to four months of it being completed for best results.

If your pile is not heating up, you'll want to add more greens (nitrogen). If your pile is starting to stink, you'll want to add more browns (carbon) and/or decrease moisture. It can take a little bit of practice and trial and error to get the mix down right, but it's a lot of fun to watch what you would normally put in the trash turn into something that can be so valuable to your yard and garden. There is no right or wrong way to compost. Use what you have and have fun with it. Remember: Compost just happens, you just have to figure out how to make it happen in a way that works for you and your set-up.

You can then add this finished compost back into your garden beds. It's a great way to be full-circle at your house. You grow the veggies, you eat them, you save the scraps, and put them into the compost pile. When the compost is ready, you add it back into the garden and start the process all over again.

Reusing Eggshells

Why have we been throwing our eggshells away for so many years when there are so many great uses for them? I now save all of mine. I absolutely love to reuse as much as I can. I find that keeping a specific bowl by or under the sink for scraps and eggshells helps remind me and the kids to not throw this useful stuff away.

Eggshells can be used in so many ways. When my bowl starts to overflow, they go in the oven at 175°F for 10 minutes to cook off all the bacteria. The eggshells then go into a food processor or blender and are ground into almost a powder. I store them in a Mason jar so they're ready for future use. You can use them in your garden to keep slugs and other pests away from your veggies, you can throw them into your compost pile or add them to your homemade dog food (pg. 268) to give your pup a boost of calcium. Another idea is to add them to your backyard chicken feed to help the hens create eggs with strong shells.

Acknowledgments

I want to first of all thank my husband, Adam, who ate many semi-cold meals for months because I needed to get photos (let's be real, several photos) of each dish before we could begin to eat. He is and always has been my biggest supporter in whatever crazy things I want to do. I want to thank my step kiddos, Asher, Kellan, and Reed, for trying all kinds of new dishes that I experimented with and for being brutally honest if they thought it tasted like crap.

Mom, thanks for always picking up the phone and answering a million questions I have about anything and everything. Thank you for always being a great role model to me growing up and teaching me how to cook, even though it took me many years to put those lessons to use.

Mammaw, thanks for always letting me help you cook at family get-togethers, even though I would take out the extra stick of butter when you weren't looking. You throw the best parties, and I will always remember those fun family gatherings at your house. I am so happy to call you my grandma, and I love you.

Thanks to my editor, Helen Martineau, for helping me get this book into complete flowing sentences with no grammatical errors. Last but not least, thank you to Ashley Little, my design wizard, for making this book look so incredibly beautiful. I can give you just about anything and you can turn it into a beautiful masterpiece.

Index

A

B

C

W

Z